Book One

Vocabulary for Enjoyment

Harold Levine

Norman Levine

Robert T. Levine

Authors of *The Joy of Vocabulary*

When ordering this book, you may specify:
either **R 430 W** or
Vocabulary for Enjoyment, Book One

Amsco School Publications, Inc.

315 Hudson Street/New York, N.Y. 10013

Authors of Vocabulary for Enjoyment

Harold Levine
Chairman Emeritus of English,
Benjamin Cardozo High School, New York

Norman Levine
Associate Professor of English,
City College of the City University of New York

Robert T. Levine
Professor of English,
North Carolina A & T State University

Other Vocabulary Books by the Authors

Vocabulary Through Pleasurable Reading, Books I, II
Vocabulary and Composition Through Pleasurable
Reading, Books III-VI
Vocabulary for the High School Student, Books A, B
Vocabulary for the High School Student
Vocabulary for the College-Bound Student
The Joy of Vocabulary

ISBN 978-0-87720-662-0

We would like you to know that in this book, when you meet a new word for the first time, you will be given enough clues so that you can discover its meaning by yourself. We are sure that you can do this because we have faith in your intelligence. We believe that you will enjoy learning vocabulary in this way.

After you have discovered the meaning of the word, you will find at least two sample sentences that will show you how to use it properly. You will then be ready to use your new word in some challenging exercises that you will probably enjoy because each of them is like a game.

As you do the interesting things this book asks you to do, four important changes will be taking place, all at about the same time:

1. You will be increasing your vocabulary.
2. You will be improving your thinking.
3. You will be becoming a better reader.
4. You will be becoming a better listener.

In addition, you will get help with your spelling, word building, and grammar, and you will have opportunities to use your new vocabulary in short compositions.

We believe that review is important. For this reason, every third lesson in this book is a review of the previous two lessons.

After you have learned a word, try to use it in your daily conversations at home, in school, and with friends, and in the writing that you do. In this way, the word will become a part of your vocabulary forever.

The book ends with a section called *Dictionary of the Words Taught in This Book*. You may use it for review, or to look up the meaning of any new word of which you may be unsure.

We hope you will enjoy learning from this book.

Harold Levine

Norman Levine

Robert T. Levine

CONTENTS

This lesson will introduce you to five useful words, and it will help you to make them a part of your vocabulary.

A Your teacher will pronounce the new words below with you. Say each word. Then write it in the blank space in your best handwriting.

alert	_alert_
incredible	_incredible_
similar	_similar_
superior	_superior_
undecided	_undecided_

B Now we are going to help you to discover what each of the new words means. Here is a pair of sentences. *Both sentences have the same meaning.*

1*a*. A lifeguard must be watchful and ready to act quickly.
1*b*. A lifeguard must be **alert.**

> **Question:** What does **alert** mean?
>
> **Answer:** **Alert** means "watchful and ready to act quickly."

Note that **alert** does the work of six words. It is good to know words like **alert** because they can help us express ourselves in fewer words.

ALERT LIFEGUARD

1

Here are four more pairs of sentences. Remember that both sentences in each pair have the same meaning. Read each pair carefully. Then write the meaning of the new word.

2a. Your story is hard to believe.
2b. Your story is **incredible.**

    Incredible means ___hard to believe___ .

3a. In one store the bicycle was $150, and in another the price was almost but not exactly the same.
3b. In one store the bicycle was $150, and in another the price was **similar.**

    Similar means ___almost but not exactly the same.___ .

4a. Flash is a better than average dog.
4b. Flash is a **superior** dog.

    Superior means ___better than average___ .

5a. Betty was not sure what to do.
5b. Betty was **undecided.**

    Undecided means ___not sure what to do.___ .

We have just met five new words. Note that each of these words describes a person, or a thing, or an animal.

    Question: What do these new words do?

    Answer: They describe:

Alert,	in sentence 1b,	describes *lifeguard* (a person).
Incredible,	in sentence 2b,	describes *story* (a thing).
Similar,	in sentence 3b,	describes *price* (a thing).
Superior,	in sentence 4b,	describes *dog* (an animal).
Undecided,	in sentence 5b,	describes *Betty* (a person).

    Question: What do we call a word that describes a person, or thing, or animal?

    Answer: An *adjective.* The new words we are learning in this lesson—**alert, incredible, similar, superior,** and **undecided**—are all adjectives.

> Note: The abbreviation for adjective is *adj.*

C *Study Your New Words*

NEW WORD	WHAT IT MEANS	HOW IT IS USED
alert (*adj.*) ə lʉrt′	watchful and ready to act quickly; wide-awake	The **alert** cook saw that the pot was going to boil over and quickly removed it from the stove. A person who is not fully **alert** is in no condition to drive.
incredible (*adj.*) in kred′ ə b'l	unbelievable; hard to believe	Many of the things that happen in fairy tales are **incredible.** Computers can give us answers with **incredible** speed.
similar (*adj.*) sim′ ə lər	almost but not exactly the same; much the same; alike, like	Janet and Jeanette are **similar** names. Milton and I get along very well because our ideas are **similar.**
superior (*adj.*) sə pir′ ē ər	better than average; very good; excellent	The Giants will be hard to beat because they are a **superior** team. Most of the pupils scored between 75 and 80, so your 92 is a **superior** mark.
undecided (*adj.*) un′ dī sīd′ id	not sure what to do; hesitant	Have you made up your mind about how to vote, or are you still **undecided?**
	not settled; not decided	The date for the picnic is **undecided.**

D Choose the word or words needed in each sentence below, and write them in the blank spaces. The first answer has been written in as a sample.

1. The ticket sellers must have been **alert** because ___**no one**___ got in without paying.

        A. many people   B. no one

Explanation: **alert** means "watchful." When ticket sellers are **alert,** no one can get in without paying.

2. The puppies are so **similar** that it is ___*hard*___ to tell one from another.

        A. hard   B. easy

3. If you do not know ___*whether to turn right or left*___ , you are **undecided.**

        A. how to swim underwater   B. whether to turn right or left

4. She made up an **incredible** story about a horse that could ___*talk like*___ a person.

        A. run faster than   B. talk like

5. My sneakers ___*lasted a long time*___ because they were made of **superior** material.

        A. lasted a long time   B. wore out very quickly

E First read the information in all of the boxes. Then answer the questions. The first question has been answered as a sample.

> Houdini had his hands handcuffed behind his back. Then, he was put into a chest that was tightly closed and thrown into the water. And yet he was able to escape.

> The average for the class was 77. Two pupils failed. Joe got 70, Marvin 75, and Nancy 86.

> Joyce looked so much like my sister that people sometimes thought she was my sister.

> Henry could not make up his mind whether to leave or to stay.

> As soon as he smelled smoke, Ramon awakened everyone, rushed them out of the house, and ran to a neighbor to telephone the fire department.

1. Who was **undecided?**   1 __Henry__

2. Who did something **incredible?**   2 __Houdini__

3. Who seemed to be a **superior** pupil?   3 __Nancy__

4. Who saved lives by being **alert?**   4 __Ramon__

5. Who was mistaken for a different but
   similar person?   5 __Joyce__

F *Do Away With Repetition.* What adjective that you learned in this lesson can replace the italicized word or words? Enter that adjective in the space at the right. The first answer has been filled in as a sample.

1. Oranges and grapefruits are much alike. Nectarines
   and peaches are *much alike,* too.   1 __similar__

2. When I learned that light travels 186,000 miles in a
   second, I couldn't believe it. It seemed *unbelievable.*   2 __incredible__

3. Players have to be wide-awake on the field, but the
   umpire must be the most *wide-awake* of all. 3 __alert__

4. She was hesitant when we asked her to join, and
   when she was asked again today she was still *hesitant.*   4 __undecided__

5. These berries are very good. Their flavor is *very good.*   5 __superior__

6. The questions you and I asked were much the same,
   and the answers we were given were *much the same,*
   also.   6 __similar__

LESSON 2 ━━━━━━━━━━━━━━━━

When you pronounce the new words below, be sure to

1. give the *ti* in **impatient** the sound of *sh*,

2. give the *g* in **legible** the sound of *j*, and

3. give the *first g* in **obliging** also the sound of *j*.

A Look at each new word. Pronounce it. Then write it neatly in the blank space.

impatient	im pā′ shənt	_____
legible	lej′ ə b'l	_____
obliging	ə blī′ jing	_____
shy	shī	_____
unruly	un ro͞o′ lē	_____

B Both sentences in each set below have the same meaning. Read them carefully. Then write the meaning of the new word.

1. Most children are not willing to put up with delay.
   Most children are **impatient.**

   Impatient means _____.

2. Your handwriting is easy to read.
   Your handwriting is **legible.**

   Legible means _____.

3. Gary is always **obliging.**
   Gary is always ready to do favors.

   Obliging means _____.

4. Jill is not at ease with other people.
   Jill is **shy.**

   Shy means _____.

5. The crowd was **unruly.**
   The crowd was hard to control.

   Unruly means _____.

6

C Study Your New Words

NEW WORD	WHAT IT MEANS	HOW IT IS USED
impatient (*adj.*) im pā′ shənt	not willing to put up with delay or bother; easily annoyed	When the line at the checkout counter did not move, some of the customers became **impatient** and left.
	eager for something to happen; restless	Everyone was **impatient** for the game to begin.
legible (*adj.*) lej′ ə b'l	easy to read; clear enough to be read; readable	Most typed reports are more **legible** than handwritten ones.
		If you make *e*'s like *i*'s and fail to cross *t*'s, your writing will not be **legible.**
obliging (*adj.*) ə blī′ jing	ready to do favors; friendly; helpful; kind	Charlene will surely lend you her notes because she is an **obliging** person.
		I would never ask Joan or Bruce for a favor. They are not too **obliging.**
shy (*adj.*) shī	not at ease with other people; bashful	Laura was glad to meet the visitors, but Eric remained in his room because he was **shy.**
	easily frightened; timid	The pigeons became less **shy** when we offered them food, and they moved closer to us.

Lesson 2 7

unruly (*adj.*)
un rōō′ lē

hard to control or manage; not obedient; disorderly

The **unruly** pupil was allowed to return to class after promising to obey the rules.

The **unruly** stream overflowed its banks.

D Choose the word or words needed in each sentence below, and write them in the blank spaces.

1. **Unruly** hair _____.

    A. will not stay in place   B. always looks neat

2. If you _____ your name, it will be more **legible**.

    A. scribble   B. print

3. A **shy** person usually _____.

    A. asks many questions   B. has little to say

4. A store that does not _____ is very **obliging.**

    A. allow exchanges or grant refunds   B. charge for gift wrapping

5. The **impatient** child would have liked to open her presents _____ her birthday cake was brought in.

    A. before   B. after

E First read the information in all of the boxes. Then answer the questions.

When George lost his wallet, Ted lent him some money to buy lunch.

Cindy was told to go back to her seat and stop annoying others, but she continued to disturb the class.

Steve always used tiny letters, so it was almost impossible to read his writing.

> Jackie rushed through her dinner in her eagerness to get back to her TV program.

> Andy stayed away from meetings because he did not feel at ease in large gatherings.

1. Who was **shy?** 1 _____

2. Who was **impatient?** 2 _____

3. Who was **obliging?** 3 _____

4. Who was **unruly?** 4 _____

5. Who was unlikely to turn in a **legible** paper? 5 _____

F *Doing Away With Repetition.* What adjective that you learned in this lesson can replace the repeated adjective? Write your answer in the blank space.

1. The audience became restless when the curtain did not go up, and with each minute it grew more *restless*. 1 _____

2. The parents of the disorderly pupil said that he was usually not *disorderly* at home. 2 _____

3. You have been most helpful. Thank you for being so *helpful*. 3 _____

4. His notes are hard to read. Judy's are much more *readable*. 4 _____

5. It is good for bashful persons to act in a play because afterwards they may be less *bashful*. 5 _____

LESSON 3 (Review)

alert	shy
impatient	similar
incredible	superior
legible	undecided
obliging	unruly

A An adjective is missing in each sentence below. Find that adjective in the above box, and fit it into the sentence in your most legible handwriting.

1. Wendy's coat and mine are so _____ that I was not surprised when she went home with my coat.

2. Arlo has been absent much less than most of his classmates, so his attendance record is _____ .

3. It is _____ that on some winter days it is warmer in Alaska than in Florida.

4. Fourteen of my classmates have signed up for the trip, six have said they are not going, and five are still _____ .

5. It was the last week of school, and everyone was _____ for the summer vacation to begin.

6. Gail used to be _____ when she was called on to read her composition to the class, but now she is much more at ease.

7. We would be glad to do you a favor because you have always been very
   _____ to us.

8. It was hard to tell to whom the paper belonged because the name on it was not too
   _____ .

9. If you are not _____ when you play checkers with Marvin, you
   may fall into a trap.

10. The meeting room was overcrowded, but everyone obeyed the regulations and no
    one was _____ .

B *Using Fewer Words.* Which adjective can take the place of the italicized expression?
Find that adjective in the box on page 10, and write it neatly in the space at the right.

1. We have taken no action because we are *not sure what
   to do.*   1 _____

2. It is difficult to choose between two candidates whose
   ideas are *much the same.*   2 _____

3. A sign is of no value unless it is *easy to read.*   3 _____

4. Young babysitters should not be left in charge of children who are *hard to manage.*   4 _____

5. The climate this past week has been *better than average.* 5 _____

6. People who are *easily annoyed* are quick to lose their
   temper.   6 _____

7. If you have heard the expression "scared as a rabbit," you must know that rabbits are *easily frightened.*   7 _____

8. To be a good basketball player you must be con-
   stantly *watchful and ready to act quickly.*   8 _____

9. Our neighbors mind their own business, and they
   are always *ready to do favors.*   9 _____

10. The excuse you gave was *hard to believe.*   10 _____

C For each partly spelled adjective below, do the following:

- In column A, enter the missing letter.
- In column B, write the complete adjective.
- In column C, write the meaning of the adjective. Take all your meanings from the WORD LIST below.

The first answer has been completed as a sample.

Column A	*Column B*	*Column C*
1. impa__t__ient child	impatient	restless
2. leg ____ ble signature		
3. sim ____ lar results		
4. obli ____ ing classmate		
5. incred ____ ble news		
6. unr ____ ly people		
7. al ____ rt mother		
8. unde ____ ided voter		
9. s ____ perior performance		
10. sh ____ newcomer		
11. impat ____ ent customer		

WORD LIST:

alike	hesitant
bashful	readable
disorderly	restless
excellent	unbelievable
friendly	wide-awake

D Consider each question carefully. When you have made up your mind, do the following:

1. Next to **Answer**, write "Yes" or "No."
2. Next to **Explanation**, give *one or more reasons* for your "Yes" or "No." A "Yes" or "No" that is not backed up by a good explanation is not worth very much.

The first question has been answered as a sample.

1. Should the whole class be punished if a few students have been unruly?

   Answer: No.

   Explanation: Only the unruly ones should be punished. It does not make sense to punish students who have done nothing wrong. It would only make them angry.

2. Do you consider yourself an obliging person?

   Answer: _____

   Explanation: _____

   _____

   _____

   _____

   _____

   _____

3. Suppose you have gotten superior marks on your tests and have not missed a day of school. Yet, when you get your report card, you notice that you have been given the same rating as everyone else in the class. Is this fair?

   Answer: _____

   Explanation: _____

   _____

   _____

   _____

   _____

   _____

E *Listening.* Your teacher will now read an interesting passage to you and give you some questions to answer. Follow your teacher's instructions.

Our first word in this lesson is **arduous** (är′ joo wəs). Note the heavy stress mark [′] after *är*. It tells us to stress *är* when we pronounce this word. Always stress the syllable that has a [′] following it.

A Pronounce each new word and write it legibly in the blank space.

arduous	är′ joo wəs	_____
boring	bôr′ ing	_____
familiar	fə mil′ yər	_____
reluctant	ri luk′ tənt	_____
timid	tim′ id	_____

Now, if you are alert, you should be able to discover the meaning of each of the new words. Let us begin with **arduous.**

Painting a room may look easy, but it is **arduous** work.

ARDUOUS

Question: What does **arduous** mean?

Answer: If you have read the above sentence carefully, you should see that **arduous** is the OPPOSITE of *easy.* **Arduous,** therefore, means **difficult,** or **not easy.**

14

B Every sentence below has a new word, like **arduous,** and an OPPOSITE word, like *easy*. Read carefully. Then answer the questions.

1. Judy is too **timid** to jump into the pool but Sharon is unafraid.

TIMID

   (*a*) Which word is the opposite of **timid?** _____

   (*b*) What does **timid** mean? _____

2. We were hoping to find at least one **familiar** person in the crowd, but we saw only strange faces.

   (*a*) Which word is the opposite of **familiar?** _____

   (*b*) What does **familiar** mean? _____

3. I wondered why you had said the movie was interesting because I found it **boring**.

   (*a*) Which word is the opposite of **boring?** _____

   (*b*) What does **boring** mean? _____

4. When you asked us to wait for you, I was willing, but our driver was **reluctant.**

   (*a*) Which word is the opposite of **reluctant?** _____

   (*b*) What does **reluctant** mean? _____

> *Note*: An opposite word is known as an ***antonym***.
> The abbreviation for antonym is *ant*.

NEW WORD	WHAT IT MEANS	HOW IT IS USED
arduous (*adj.*) är′ joo wəs	hard to do; difficult *ant.* **easy**	Adding long columns of numbers without a calculator is an **arduous** task.
	using up a great deal of energy; strenuous	If running is too **arduous** for you, try jogging.
boring (*adj.*) bôr′ ing	tiresome and uninteresting; dull *ant.* **interesting**	My vacation was so **boring** that I was glad when it was over. No one likes to listen to a **boring** speech.
familiar (*adj.*) fə mil′ yər	well-known; easily recognized; common *ant.* **strange**	Skyscrapers are a **familiar** sight to those who live in big cities.
	well acquainted; having a good knowledge of	I am not **familiar** with this machine. Please show me how to operate it.
reluctant (*adj.*) ri luk′ tənt	unwilling; slow to act because of unwillingness; not inclined *ant.* **willing**	We had such a good time at the party that we were **reluctant** to leave. The prices were too high, so people were **reluctant** to buy.
timid (*adj.*) tim′ id	easily frightened; feeling or showing fear or shyness; afraid *ant.* **unafraid; fearless**	When the magician asked for a volunteer, Walter went up on the stage. He is not **timid.** If Martha had been more sure of her answer, she would not have given it in such a **timid** voice.

D Choose the word or words needed, and write them in the blank spaces.

1. Taking the elevator is ＿＿＿＿＿＿＿ **arduous** than climbing the stairs.

    A. more   B. less

2. A person who is always **reluctant** to do a favor is ＿＿＿＿＿＿＿＿＿ to be a good friend.

    A. unlikely   B. likely

3. Dinner becomes **boring** if ＿＿＿＿＿＿＿＿＿＿＿＿＿＿＿＿＿＿＿＿ is served every evening.

    A. the same food   B. something different

4. **Timid** customers ＿＿＿＿＿＿＿＿＿＿＿＿＿＿＿＿＿＿＿＿＿.

    A. do not let themselves be   B. are unwilling to make
       cheated   complaints

5. ＿＿＿＿＿＿＿＿＿＿＿＿＿＿＿ are expected to be **familiar** with the city's streets.

    A. Out-of-towners   B. City taxi drivers

E Each set of facts below is followed by a question. Consider the facts carefully before answering the question. The first question has been answered as a sample.

1. FACTS: Eva has been to Palm Beach once, Virginia Beach twice, and Jones Beach many times.

    Question: Which of the three beaches is Eva most familiar with?
    Answer: **Jones Beach.**

2. FACTS: Today Andy met Nancy, who talked only about herself. He also met Yong, who thanked him for a favor, and Joe, who gave him some important news.

    Question: Who was probably the most boring person that Andy met today?
    Answer: ＿＿＿＿＿＿＿＿＿＿＿＿＿＿＿＿＿＿＿＿＿＿＿＿

3. FACTS: Before leaving, Harriet had to clean her room, take in the mail, and turn off the air-conditioning.

> **Question:** What was the most arduous thing that Harriet had to do before leaving?
>
> **Answer:** _____

4. FACTS: Rita, Ben, and Carolyn all refused to take part in the play—Rita because she could not get the part she wanted, Ben because he was afraid he would forget his lines, and Carolyn because she had just come out of the hospital.

> **Question:** Who was timid about something?
>
> **Answer:** _____

5. FACTS: Jim said he would take charge of the equipment if we wanted him to, or act as scorekeeper, but he would not serve as umpire unless we could not find anyone else to do the job.

> **Question:** What was Jim reluctant to do?
>
> **Answer:** _____

6. FACTS: Ronnie usually plays first base. He has also had some experience at third base and in the outfield, but he has never played shortstop.

> **Question:** What position is Ronnie least familiar with?
>
> **Answer:** _____

F *Using Fewer Words.* What adjective that you learned in this lesson can take the place of the italicized words? Enter that adjective in the blank space.

1. Most animals are *easily frightened*.   1 _____

2. I turned off the program because it was *tiresome and uninteresting*.   2 _____

3. We cannot understand why you are *not willing* to try out for the team.   3 _____

4. Are you *well acquainted* with the rules of the game?   4 _____

5. I did not find the work too *hard to do*.   5 _____

 *LESSON* 5

Artificial (är′ tə fish′ əl) has two stress marks—a light one [′] after *är* and a heavy one [′] after *fish*. When we say this word, we stress *är* lightly, but give the main stress to *fish*.

A Pronounce each new word and write it legibly in the blank space.

artificial	är′ tə fish′ əl	_____
awkward	ôk′ wərd	_____
negligent	neg′ li jənt	_____
permanent	pʉr′ mə nənt	_____
scarce	skers	_____

Now see if you can discover what each of the new words means. Let us begin with **negligent.**

We would rather ride with a careful driver than a **negligent** one.

Question: What does **negligent** mean?

Answer: Obviously, a **negligent** driver is the OPPOSITE of a *careful* driver.

Negligent, then, means *careless*, or *not careful*.

B Each sentence below contains a possibly strange word, like **negligent**, and a familiar OPPOSITE word, like *careful*. Read carefully. Then answer the questions.

1. On my next visit, the dentist will replace my temporary filling with a **permanent** one.

    (*a*) Which word is the opposite of **permanent?** _____

    (*b*) What does **permanent** mean? _____

2. The mechanic was skillful but his helper was hopelessly **awkward.**

    (*a*) Which word is the opposite of **awkward?** _____

    (*b*) What does **awkward** mean? _____

ARTIFICIAL LIGHT

3. Natural daylight is better for reading than the **artificial** light of lamps.

   (*a*) Which word is the opposite of **artificial?** _____

   (*b*) What does **artificial** mean? _____

4. Fresh vegetables cost less when they are plentiful and more when they are **scarce.**

   (*a*) Which word is the opposite of **scarce?** _____

   (*b*) What does **scarce** mean? _____

C Study Your New Words

NEW WORD	WHAT IT MEANS	HOW IT IS USED
artificial (*adj.*) är′ tə fish′ əl	not natural; made by human beings rather than nature *ant.* **natural**	I would never have thought the flowers were **artificial** because they looked so natural.
	false; pretended; not sincere	When people greet you with an **artificial** smile, you can tell they are not overjoyed to see you.
awkward (*adj.*) ôk′ wərd	not skillful; not graceful; clumsy *ant.* **skillful; graceful**	With coaching, an **awkward** batter can become a skillful hitter.
	difficult; uncomfortable; embarrassing	My neighbors saw me as I was searching for my ball in their flower garden. It was an **awkward** situation.

negligent *(adj.)* neg′ li jənt	failing to use proper care; careless *ant.* **careful**	I dialed the wrong number because I was **negligent.** I should have paid more attention to what I was doing. Fires are often caused by **negligent** smokers who fail to put out their cigarettes.
permanent *(adj.)* pur′ mə nənt	not temporary; lasting or meant to last for a very long time *ant.* **temporary**	Right now I do babysitting, but I do not expect it to be my **permanent** occupation. The Pilgrims left England and lived for a time in Holland before finding a **permanent** home in America.
scarce *(adj.)* skers	hard to get; not plentiful; not abundant *ant.* **abundant**	Water is **scarce** in countries where there is not enough rainfall. Many shoppers buy frozen or canned spinach when fresh spinach is **scarce.**

D Choose the words needed in each sentence below, and write them in the blank spaces.

1. _____ provide **artificial** light.

    A. Candles and flashlights   B. The stars

2. Coffee is **scarce** when there is a _____ in Brazil.

    A. record crop   B. crop failure

3. It is **awkward** to _____.

    A. hit your thumb while using a hammer   B. eat soup with a spoon

4. The people who _____ in the seashore village are its **permanent** residents.

    A. live all year   B. spend their vacations

5. You are **negligent** if you _____

_____.

    A. close the windows in your room when the air-conditioning is on   B. always have to be reminded to fasten your seat belt

E   *Using Fewer Words.* What adjective that you learned in this lesson can take the place of the italicized word or words? Write that adjective in the blank space.

1. My brother thought that his assignment to the mail room would be temporary, but he soon learned that it was *not temporary*.

1 _____

2. If lettuce is *hard to get*, you can buy some celery instead.

2 _____

3. I nearly dropped a whole tray of dishes. I was so *clumsy*.

3 _____

4. Each driver accused the other of carelessness, but the fact is that both were *careless*.

4 _____

5. Cotton, wool, and silk are natural fibers. Rayon, nylon, dacron, and orlon are *not natural*.

5 _____

F   Each set of facts below is followed by a question. Consider the facts carefully before answering.

1. FACTS: A member of the House of Representatives is elected for a term of two years. A Supreme Court Justice serves for life. A President is elected for a term of four years.

    Question: Which of the three public officials mentioned above holds a permanent position?

    Answer: _____

2. FACTS: The following were advertised for sale in a daily newspaper:

        For $39,000, a Mercedes automobile less than a year old.
        For $1700, a Yamaha motorcycle four years old.
        For $35,000, a baseball autographed in 1929 by Babe Ruth, the famous home-run hitter.

Question: Which of the advertised articles is probably the most scarce?

Answer: _____

3. FACTS: Yesterday, in her English class, Lola got permission to make her report on Monday, instead of tomorrow. At lunch, she spilled half of her soup as she carried it from the counter to her table. In gym, she won the 50-yard dash, but came in third in the foul-shooting contest.

Question: What was the most awkward thing that Lola did yesterday?

Answer: _____

_____

4. FACTS: Ruth bought a wool sweater for Mom, a nylon shirt for Dad, and cotton jeans for Max, and all of them thanked her for the gifts.

Question: Which of these gifts was made of artificial material?

Answer: _____

5. FACTS: Juan was the first to hand in his science test paper. The teacher had to call Juan back, though, because he had forgotten to write his name on the paper. On this test, only two students scored 100%, and one of them was Juan.

Question: In what way was Juan negligent?

Answer: _____

_____

LESSON 6 (Review)

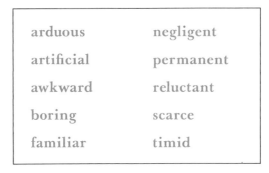

arduous	negligent
artificial	permanent
awkward	reluctant
boring	scarce
familiar	timid

A An adjective is missing in each sentence below. Find that adjective in the above list, and write it in the blank space.

1. The first story held my interest, but the second was _____.

2. Paul never asks questions in class when he does not understand something because he is as _____ as a rabbit.

3. I enjoyed the book so much that I was _____ to put it down.

4. A(n) _____ shopper left her purse on the counter, and the salesclerk had to run after her to return it.

5. My sister and her boyfriend are taking dancing lessons because they do not want to look _____ on the ballroom floor.

6. The Panama Canal is a(n) _____ waterway, since it was built by human beings rather than nature.

7. My part-time job was so _____ that it wore me out.

8. It was feared that the patient's loss of speech would be _____ , but fortunately it lasted only a couple of days.

9. There are plenty of blueberries now, as they are in season, but in a few weeks they will be _____ and much more expensive.

10. I was _____ with the joke that you told because I had heard it before.

B *Using Fewer Words.* Which adjective can take the place of the italicized expression? Find that adjective in the box on page 24, and write it neatly in the space at the right, as in the following sample:

flavor *that is not natural*   **artificial** _____ flavor

1. exercise *that uses up a great deal of energy*   1 _____ exercise

2. workers *who fail to use the proper care*   2 _____ workers

3. songs *that are easily recognized*   3 _____ songs

4. people *who are afraid or shy*   4 _____ people

5. helpers *who are slow to help because of unwillingness*   5 _____ helpers

6. Jobs were *hard to get.*   6 Jobs were _____.

7. games *that are tiresome and uninteresting*   7 _____ games

8. laughter *that is not sincere*   8 _____ laughter

9. improvements *that are meant to last for a very long time*   9 _____ improvements

10. situation *that is uncomfortable or embarrassing*   10 _____ situation

C For each partly spelled adjective below, do the following:

- In column A, enter the missing letter.
- In column B, write the complete adjective.
- In column C, write an ANTONYM of that adjective. Take all your antonyms from the WORD LIST at the end of this exercise.

The first answer has been completed as a sample.

Column A	*Column B*	*Column C*
1. **famil** _i_ **ar** surroundings	familiar	strange
2. **tim** ____ **d** reply		
3. **ard** ____ **ous** task		
4. **scar** ____ **e** supplies		
5. **artific** ____ **al** flowers		
6. **reluct** ____ **nt** witness		
7. **b** ____ **ring** afternoon		
8. **a** ____ **kward** dancer		
9. **perm** ____ **nent** address		
10. **negl** ____ **gent** guard		
11. **famili** ____ **r** excuse		

WORD LIST:

abundant	interesting
careful	natural
easy	strange
fearless	temporary
graceful	willing

D Consider each question carefully. Then do the following:

     1. Next to **Answer,** write "Yes" or "No."
     2. Next to **Explanation,** give one or more *good reasons* for your "Yes" or "No."

1. A classmate who borrowed your pen was negligent about returning it. You almost had to beg to get it back. Would you lend that classmate anything again?

Answer: _____

Explanation: _____

_____

_____

_____

_____

2. Would you like to have natural plants in your home rather than artificial ones?

Answer: _____

Explanation: _____

_____

_____

_____

_____

3. One of the best players in your group wants to be captain all the time. Should that player be made the permanent captain?

Answer: _____

Explanation: _____

_____

_____

_____

_____

E *Listening.* Your teacher will now read an interesting passage to you and give you some questions to answer. Follow your teacher's instructions.

LESSON 7 ━━━━━━━━━━━━━━

Do you realize that you are not just one person but many? For example, in addition to being a *boy* or a *girl,* you are also a *son* or a *daughter,* a *student,* a *reader,* a *listener,* a *friend,* a *neighbor,* a *customer,* a *passenger,* an *American,* etc., etc.

This lesson will deal with some of the people you already are or may become.

Pronunciation:

> The *o* in **host** and **hostess** is pronounced *o,* as in *go.*
> But the *o* in **novice** and **optimist** is pronounced *ä,* as in *lot.*

A Pronounce each new word. Then write it neatly.

dependent	di pen′ dənt	_____
guest	gest	_____
host	hōst	_____
hostess	hōs′ tis	_____
novice	näv′ is	_____
optimist	äp′ tə mist	_____

Perhaps you are already familiar with some of the new words. Here, then, is a chance to show what you may already know about them. It is called a *preview.*

B *Preview:* Fill each blank space with the right word from the above box. You can check your answers in the next section. The first answer has been filled in as a sample.

1. When you are invited to a party and you go there, you are a(n) ____**guest**____.

2. If Luther is giving the party, he is the _____ .

3. If Jennifer is giving the party, she is the _____ .

4. You are a(n) _____ if you always think that everything will turn out all right.

5. When you are able to earn a living and no longer need to be supported, you will stop being a(n) _____ .

6. If you are just beginning to learn to dance, you are a(n) _____ in dancing.

Note that the new words in this lesson—**dependent, guest, host, hostess, novice,** and **optimist**—are *words that name persons*. Such words are called *nouns*. The abbreviation for noun is *n.*

C Study Your New Words

NEW WORD	WHAT IT MEANS	HOW IT IS USED
dependent (*n.*) di pen′ dənt	person who is supported by someone else	If you do not support yourself, you are a **dependent.**

My brother and his wife have just become the parents of twins, so they have two new **dependents.**

guest (*n.*) gest	person entertained in another person's home; visitor	Gloria will be my **guest** on Saturday. She is coming to my house for lunch.
	person treated to a meal or other entertainment	When someone invites you to a theater or a restaurant, you are not expected to pay because you are a **guest.**

host (*n.*) hōst hostess (*n.*) hōs′ tis	person who entertains guests at home, or pays for their entertainment at a restaurant or theater	A good **host** or **hostess** tries to make the guests feel welcome.
	Note that **host** is used for a male, and **hostess** for a female.	Mr. and Mrs. Smith have invited us. He is a witty **host,** and she is a very kind **hostess.**
novice (*n.*) näv′ is	person who is new at something; beginner *ant.* **expert**	Enid is an **expert** in bowling, so she will teach me. I am just a **novice.** It is not usual for a champion in a sport to be defeated by a **novice.**
optimist (*n.*) äp′ tə mist	person who is cheerful and believes that everything will turn out all right *ant.* **pessimist**	The coach, who is an **optimist,** expects us to win. But my sister, who is a **pessimist,** says we will lose. Chen lost his watch, but he is sure someone will find it and return it to him. He is an **optimist.**

Reminder: At this time, correct any mistakes you may have made in the preview.

D Which choice is better, *A* or *B*? Write the words of your answer in the blank space.

1. Before an examination, **pessimists** usually feel that they are going to _____ .

    A. pass   B. fail

2. _____ of the pupils in a kindergarten class are **dependents.**

    A. All   B. None

3. I played racquetball with a **novice** who _____
   of the game.

    A. didn't even know the rules   B. showed me some of the tricks

4. It is usually _____ to be a guest than a **host** or **hostess.**

    A. easier   B. harder

5. **Optimists** _____ that a cure for cancer can be found.

    A. doubt   B. believe

E   Read the statements in all of the boxes. Then answer the questions below.

We have won our first two games, and already Nora is saying that we will win the championship.

Today's meeting is in Harvey's house. He will serve refreshments.	Jill has begun taking piano lessons with a private teacher, and she practices every day.

Tony expects to begin working when he is 18 because he does not want his parents to support him forever.	Ann is going to Ruby's party at the Village Inn, and she is bringing Ruby a book as a present.

Hattie says she has never won anything and never will, so she will not buy a raffle ticket.

    1. Who is an **optimist?**   1 _____

    2. Who is a **novice?**   2 _____

    3. Who seems reluctant to be a **dependent?**   3 _____

    4. Who is a **host?**   4 _____

    5. Who is a **hostess?**   5 _____

    6. Who is a **pessimist?**   6 _____

    7. Who is a **guest?**   7 _____

F *Using Fewer Words.* Replace each italicized expression below with a noun that you studied in this lesson.

1. You cannot get much encouragement from a(n) *person who always expects that the worst is going to happen.*

   1 _____

2. A(n) *person who is new to a field* has a great deal to learn.

   2 _____

3. A(n) *person who is entertained at someone else's home* usually receives a hearty welcome.

   3 _____

4. Almost every *person supported by someone else* is eager to earn his or her own living as soon as possible.

   4 _____

5. The bill for the party at the restaurant was paid by the *man who invited the guests.*

   5 _____

6. In magic shows, Debra is the *person with special knowledge and experience*, not I.

   6 _____

7. Annie is a(n) *person who believes that everything will turn out all right.*

   7 _____

A Pronounce each new word and write it neatly. Note:

The *o* in **adolescent** is weak and is pronounced ə, like the *o* in *collect*.

adolescent	ad′ ə les′′nt	_____
culprit	kul′ prit	_____
pedestrian	pə des′ trē ən	_____
rival	rī′ v'l	_____
victor	vik′ tər	_____

Now do the preview. It will give you a chance to show what you may already know about the new words.

B *Preview:* Fill each blank below with the word from the above box that in your opinion is the best choice. You can check your answers in the next section.

1. The Republican candidate got only forty-one votes more than her Democratic

   _____.

2. Almost everyone enrolled in the seventh grade is, or is about to become, a(n)

   _____.

3. At a crossing, a driver should give the right of way to a(n) _____.

4. We blamed Lew, but later we discovered that Ida was the real _____.

5. After the match, the _____ and the loser shook hands.

NEW WORD	WHAT IT MEANS	HOW IT IS USED
adolescent (*n.*) ad' ə les' 'nt	person between childhood and adulthood; teenager	Lori, who is 13, is not the only **adolescent** in the family. Her sister Lynne is 16, and her brother Roger is 19. The guests at the party were all under 10, so it would have been boring for an **adolescent.**
culprit (*n.*) kul' prit	person who has committed a fault or crime; offender	Someone took my eraser. Are you the **culprit?** Two people were killed in the crash, but the **culprit,** a drunken driver, was not seriously hurt.
pedestrian (*n.*) pə des' trē ən	person who goes on foot; walker	If you ride your bicycle on a crowded sidewalk, you may hit a **pedestrian.** On our early morning walk we saw several joggers, but we were the only **pedestrians.**
rival (*n.*) rī' v'l	person who tries to do better than another, or strives for a goal that only one can reach; competitor	Holly was elected because she made better speeches and had more posters than her **rival.** Dominick crossed the finish line a full second ahead of his nearest **rival.**

victor (*n.*)	person who wins a	I usually beat Carmen in
vik′ tər	contest, struggle, or	chess, but today she was
	battle; winner	the **victor.**
	ant. **loser**	

Thomas E. Dewey seemed to have won the 1948 election for President, but the final count showed that the **victor** was Harry S. Truman.

Reminder: Correct any mistakes you may have made in the preview.

D Below are two ways for completing each sentence. Choose the way that fits the sentence, and write the words of your answer in the blank space.

1. There is no **victor** in a game that ends in a score of _____ .

    A. 1-1   B. 7-0

2. It usually takes a **pedestrian** _____ time than a car driver to travel between cities.

    A. less   B. more

3. A candidate who has no **rival** is sure to be _____ .

    A. defeated   B. elected

4. It makes no sense to _____ **culprits.**

    A. reward   B. punish

5. A father who supports his wife and their three children has _____ **dependents.**

    A. four   B. three

E Each set of facts below is followed by a question. Consider the facts carefully before answering.

1. FACTS: Andrew was driven to the game by his parents; Cathy arrived late because she missed the bus and had to walk all the way; and Warren came on his bicycle.

    Question: Who was a pedestrian?

    Answer: _____

2. FACTS: Ellen and Bruce each had their own lemonade stands about 100 feet apart.

Since Peter was the only one who wanted to be scorekeeper, we allowed him to take that responsibility.

Both Dorothy and Yoko asked to operate the copying machine, so the teacher said they should take turns.

Question: Who had no rival?

Answer: _____

3. FACTS: In the final race Larry had an early lead but could not hold it. Umberto, despite a pebble in his shoe, finished first, a split second ahead of Bruce.

Question: Who was the victor?

Answer: _____

4. FACTS: Bill's letter was returned to him by the post office because he had forgotten to put a stamp on it.

Ted did not show his report card to his mother, and in the space where she was supposed to sign, he wrote her name.

Millie accidentally handed the toll collector a nickel, instead of a quarter.

Question: Who was the worst culprit?

Answer: _____

5. FACTS: Vivian is eight, Scott is fourteen and a half, and Diane will be sixteen next month.

Question: Who is not an adolescent?

Answer: _____

F *Using Fewer Words.* Replace the italicized expression with a noun that you studied in this lesson.

1. When traffic is jammed, a(n) *person who goes on foot* can
   make better progress than a taxicab passenger.   1 _____

2. The *person who won the contest* was overjoyed. 2 _____

3. When you have a(n) *person who is trying to do better than you,* you have to work harder to get ahead. 3 _____

4. The *person who committed the crime* left no fingerprints. 4 _____

5. The assistant manager looked like a(n) *person in his teens.* 5 _____

G Two words are missing in each passage below. Choose those words from the following list and enter them in the blank spaces. Do not use any of these words more than once.

adolescent	familiar
alert	impatient
arduous	loser
competitor	pedestrian
culprit	shy

The first passage has been completed as a sample.

1. The victor was in no hurry to play another game, but the __loser__ was __impatient__ .

2. Yolanda, who had been _____ as a child, grew out of her bashfulness before she became a(n) _____ .

3. The _____ would not have had a chance to escape if the guards had been more _____ .

4. On my way to the bus stop, I noticed a(n) _____ walking toward me who looked _____ , but he turned out to be a stranger.

5. Quentin crossed the finish line barely a split second before his nearest _____ . Both of them were out of breath. It had been a(n) _____ race.

LESSON   9 (Review) ━━━◆━◆━◆━◆━━━

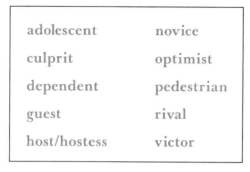

adolescent	novice
culprit	optimist
dependent	pedestrian
guest	rival
host/hostess	victor

A A noun is missing in each passage below. Find that noun in the above list, and write it in the blank space.

1. The _____ in tonight's bout will be recognized as the world champion.

2. A(n) _____ is anyone from an infant to an elderly person who is supported by someone else.

3. Dan says we don't have a chance, but Rose believes we'll succeed. She's a(n) _____ .

4. Charges against Farrell will be dropped now that the true _____ has confessed.

5. So far, you are the only candidate for treasurer. If no one else is nominated you will have no _____ for that job.

6. I did not have to pay for my ticket since Elliott had invited me to the theater as his _____ .

7. When you enter college, you will probably still be a(n) _____ , but by the time you graduate you will be an adult.

8. Angela applied her brakes to avoid hitting a(n) _____ who suddenly darted across the road.

9. If you want me to bowl with you, you will have to teach me because I am a(n) _____ .

10. The _____ was worried because it was time for dinner and two of her guests had not yet arrived.

B One letter is missing in each noun below. Write the missing letter in the space where it belongs. Then write the complete noun.

vict __ r _____ h __ st _____

pedestr __ an _____ culpr __ t _____

host __ ss _____ pessim __ st _____

depend __ nt _____ novi __ e _____

riv __ l _____ g __ est _____

optim __ st _____ adoles __ ent _____

C Next to each expression below, write a noun that can take its place. Choose your nouns from the above box.

1. person who goes on foot 1 _____

2. man who entertains guests 2 _____

3. person who believes everything will turn out all right 3 _____

4. person who has committed a fault or crime 4 _____

5. person entertained in another's home 5 _____

6. person supported by someone else 6 _____

7. woman who entertains guests 7 _____

8. person who expects nothing will turn out all right 8 _____

9. person who is new at something 9 _____

10. person who strives for a goal that only one can reach 10 _____

11. person between childhood and adulthood 11 _____

12. person who wins a contest, struggle, or battle 12 _____

D An adjective is needed in each sentence below. Find that adjective in the list at the end of this exercise, and write it into the sentence. The first sentence has been completed as a sample.

1. Pat was tired from the long and ____arduous____ campaign, but she was happy to be the victor.

2. If the champion were to lose to a novice, it would be _____ .

3. There were no strangers at the party since all the guests were _____ with one another.

4. The culprit responsible for the forest fire was a smoker who was _____ in disposing of a cigarette.

5. Joe is 24, but he is still living with his parents as a dependent because he is _____ to go to work.

6. The _____ pedestrian started to cross the street before the light had changed to green.

7. As the guests were leaving, it began to rain, so the _____ host offered to drive them home.

8. I voted for Ellen, instead of her rival, because Ellen has a(n) _____ record.

9. Annie never gave up her cheerfulness, even temporarily, and for that reason we may consider her a(n) _____ optimist.

10. Jasper, who was bashful as a child, is much less _____ as an adolescent.

LIST OF ADJECTIVES (Write in the two missing letters before moving the adjective up to the sentence where it is needed.)

ard _u_ _o_ us	ob __ __ ging
p __ __ manent	fa __ __ liar
impa __ __ ent	rel __ __ tant
incre __ __ ble	__ __ y
__ __ perior	n __ __ ligent

E Consider each question carefully. Then do the following:

1. Next to **Answer,** write "Yes" or "No."
2. Next to **Explanation,** give one or more *good reasons* for your "Yes" or "No."

1. Two friends who are frequent guests in your home have never invited you to their homes. Would you nevertheless continue to invite these friends?

Answer: _____

Explanation: _____

_____

_____

_____

_____

2. Is it fair for an adolescent to be paid less than an adult who does the same work?

Answer: _____

Explanation: _____

_____

_____

_____

_____

3. The courts have been giving much lighter sentences to teenage culprits than to older criminals. Is this wise?

Answer: _____

Explanation: _____

_____

_____

_____

_____

F *Listening.* Your teacher will now read an interesting passage to you and give you some questions to answer. Follow your teacher's instructions.

LESSON 10

A Pronounce each new word. Then write it neatly. Note:

The *ei* in **leisure** is pronounced *ē*, as in *be*.

The *s* in **leisure** is pronounced *zh*, as in *pleasure*.

The *s* in **reservoir** is pronounced *z*, as in *lazy*.

blunder	blun′ dər	_____
fragment	frag′ mənt	_____
intersection	in′ tər sek′ shən	_____
leisure	lē′ zhər	_____
reservoir	rez′ ər vwär	_____

B *Preview*: Fill each blank below with the word from the above box that you think is the best choice.

1. I thought I had picked up all the broken pieces of the mirror you dropped yesterday, but I just found another _____ .

2. My friends and I have very little _____ this week because we are busy preparing for our examinations.

3. Gail took the wrong bus. I once made that _____ , too.

4. There is a traffic light at the busy _____ of Main Street and Lewis Avenue.

5. The town's _____ is almost empty, so people are being asked not to water their lawns.

42

> *Note*: We have already learned that words that name persons (**guest, rival**, etc.) are nouns.
>
> Words that name things (**blunder, fragment, leisure**) are nouns, too.
>
> And so, too, are words that name places (**intersection, reservoir**).
>
> A **noun** is usually defined as a *word that names a person, place, or thing.*

C Study Your New Words

NEW WORD	WHAT IT MEANS	HOW IT IS USED
blunder (*n.*) blun′ dər	careless or foolish mistake; error	The new member's name was Bill, but I kept calling him "Bob" until someone told me of my **blunder**. The salesclerk made a **blunder** and gave me a dollar too much, but I gave it back to her.
fragment (*n.*) frag′ mənt	part broken off from a whole; small piece	In a corner, I found a **fragment** of the shattered glass pitcher. Betty broke her crackers into **fragments** and put them into her soup.

intersection (n.) in' tər sek' shən	place where two or more things—for example, streets—cross; crossing	The gas station at the **intersection** of Broadway and Joyce Road is open 24 hours a day.
		A very young child needs to be accompanied by an adult when crossing a dangerous **intersection.**
leisure (n.) lē' zhər	free time; time to do the things you like to do	Anyone who has a part-time job in addition to a regular job has very little **leisure.**
		It is a mistake to spend all of your **leisure** watching TV.
reservoir (n.) rez' ər vwär	place where water is collected and stored for use	The recent heavy rains have almost filled the town's **reservoir.**
	place where anything is collected and stored	Computers are **reservoirs** of facts and information.

D Which choice makes the sentence correct, *A* or *B?* Write the words of your answer in the blank space.

1. The average person has _____ **leisure** on weekends than at any other time of the week.

  A. less   B. more

2. Fortunately, I did not _____ my **blunder.**

  A. correct   B. repeat

3. At most **intersections,** there is traffic coming from _____ directions.

  A. four   B. two

4. I had to sweep up the **fragments** after I dropped _____.

  A. a handful of coins   B. an electric light bulb

5. If people waste water, there is a danger that the **reservoirs** may _____.

  A. overflow   B. run dry

E Read the statements in all the boxes. Then answer the questions below.

Angela, our new neighbor, used to live at the corner of State Street and Garrison Avenue.

When Perry finished watering his vegetable garden, he took a dip in his backyard swimming pool.

Audrey found the school closed when she got there. She had completely forgotten it was a holiday.

Right after her two-month vacation in Hawaii, Donna left on a six-week cruise around the world.

For months after the garage was built, Carl kept picking up bits of construction material from the nearby grass.

1. Who collected **fragments?**   1 _____

2. Who moved from an **intersection?**   2 _____

3. Who seemed to have the most **leisure?** 3 _____

4. Who committed a **blunder?**   4 _____

5. Who seemed to be making special demands on the community **reservoir?**   5 _____

F *Using Fewer Words.* Replace the italicized expression below with a noun that you studied in this lesson.

1. The accident occurred at a(n) *place where two streets cross.*

   1 _____

2. It was a(n) *foolish mistake* for you to interfere in the quarrel between the two rivals.

   2 _____

3. If each family had its own well, the town would not need a(n) *place for collecting and storing water.*

   3 _____

4. Next summer, I hope to have more *time to do the things I like to do.*

   4 _____

5. The only storm damage at our house was a(n) *small piece* of roofing material blown away by the wind.

   5 _____

G Two words are missing in each passage below. Choose those words from the following list and enter them in the blank spaces. Do not use any of these words more than once.

blunder	intersection
boring	leisure
familiar	natural
fragment	permanent

1. I thought the fur coat the actress was wearing was _____ , but it was not. It was artificial. I was not the only one who made that _____ .

2. A(n) _____ of the cherry pie fell on Perry's shirt, leaving a stain. Fortunately, he was able to wash out the stain. It was not _____ .

3. I left as soon as I could because the party was _____ , and I thought I could find a more interesting way to spend what was left of my _____ .

4. Almost everyone _____ with New York City knows that Broadway, Forty-second Street, and Seventh Avenue cross each other at a(n) _____ _____ called Times Square.

A Pronounce each new word and write it legibly. Note:

The *i* in **horizon** is pronouned $\bar{\imath}$, as in *ice*.

But the first *i* in **victim** is pronounced *i*, as in *hit*.

horizon	hə rī′ z'n	_____
mood	mōod	_____
rumor	rōo′ mər	_____
valley	val′ ē	_____
victim	vik′ təm	_____

B *Preview:* Fill each blank below with the word from the above box that, in your opinion, is the best choice.

1. I heard a report that you are going to move. Is it a fact or a(n) _____?

2. Until her bicycle was stolen yesterday, Ann had never been the _____ of a robbery.

3. We watched the tanker move out to sea until it dipped below the _____.

4. The melting mountain snows arc filling the reservoirs in the _____ below.

5. Because of his blunder on the playing field, Jack was in a bad _____ for the rest of the day.

47

NEW WORD	WHAT IT MEANS	HOW IT IS USED
horizon (*n.*) hə rī′ z'n	line where the sky seems to meet the earth or the sea	No one can see beyond the **horizon.**
	limit of a person's knowledge, experience, or outlook	Reading broadens a person's **horizon.**
mood (*n.*) mōod	state of mind (the way a person feels); disposition	Sally is in a cheerful **mood** because her vacation starts tomorrow.
		We lost because of a close play that the umpire called against us, and that put us in a bad **mood.**
rumor (*n.*) rōo′ mər	story or statement circulating from one person to another without proof as to its truth; unconfirmed report; hearsay	The mayor's absence from an important meeting led to a **rumor** that he was very ill.
		After the explosion, there was a **rumor** that several people had been killed, but it later proved to be completely untrue.
valley (*n.*) val′ ē	area of low land between hills or mountains	As you leave the mountains, the road slopes downward toward the **valley.**
		When the snow melts in the mountains, it swells the streams and rivers in the **valleys** below.

victim (*n.*) vik′ təm	person who is injured or killed	One of the **victims** of the hit-and-run driver is still in the hospital.
	person badly treated or cheated	When there is dishonesty in government, the people are the **victims.**

D Which choice makes the sentence correct, *A* or *B*? Write the words of your answer in the blank space.

1. A person who has just _____ is not likely to be in a good **mood.**

   A. gotten an award   B. missed a bus

2. The best way to deal with a **rumor** is to _____

   _____ .

   A. check to see whether or not   B. disregard it completely
        it is true

3. It is _____ to grow crops in **valleys** than on mountainsides.

   A. harder   B. easier

4. Pedestrians who cross an intersection _____ the light are more likely to become accident **victims.**

   A. against   B. with

5. As we advance towards the **horizon,** it moves _____ us.

   A. away from   B. closer to

E Each set of facts is followed by a question. Consider the facts carefully before answering.

1. FACTS: Peggy came down with the flu. Her sister Maureen and brother Raymond worried that they would catch it from her. Raymond did.

       Question: Who was not a victim?

       Answer: _____

2. FACTS: From the shore, Jack saw a tanker heading out to sea. Looking up from her garden, Rachel saw snow on the surrounding mountains. Looking down from the mountain he had climbed, Larry saw a river hundreds of feet below that looked like a silvery ribbon.

       Question: Who was in a valley?

       Answer: _____

3. FACTS: Last summer, Edna slept late and got plenty of rest, Amy learned to swim and took a beginner's course in computer science, and Janet rode her bicycle and walked her dog.

       Question: Who greatly broadened her horizons?

       Answer: _____

4. FACTS: Someone—it was not known exactly who—had said that the pool was closed. Ben immediately decided to go to the beach. Bob went down to the pool anyhow, hoping that the report he had heard was not true. Ted telephoned the pool office and asked the person in charge whether the pool was open.

       Question: Who dealt with the rumor in the most intelligent way?

       Answer: _____

5. FACTS: Marilyn discovered that she was getting a small part in the play. The part she had set her heart on was given to Mildred. John, too, was not given the part he had asked for, but he said it would be fun.

       Question: Who was probably not in a good mood?

       Answer: _____

F *Using Fewer Words.* Replace the italicized expression below with a noun that you studied in this lesson.

1. The name of the *person who was injured* has not yet been released.

1 _____

2. I heard a(n) *unconfirmed report* that the bus drivers were on strike.

2 _____

3. When you spoke to me, I was tired, hungry, and irritable. Now, I am in a better *frame of mind*.

3 _____

4. There are several farmhouses in the *area of low land between the hills*.

4 _____

5. The moon is sinking below the *point where the sky and earth seem to meet*.

5 _____

G Two words are missing in each passage below. Choose those words from the following list and enter them in the blank spaces. Do not use any of these words more than once.

adolescent	rumor
dependent	undecided
mood	valley
reluctant	victim

1. Yesterday, when Clarence wanted to play basketball, I was very tired and in no

_____ for exercise. Today, when I wanted to play, he was

_____ to leave the program he was watching.

2. We still do not know whether the story that the theater is going out of business is a

fact or just a(n) _____ . The matter remains _____ .

3. Baxter lives in a mountain cabin. He has one _____ , his eighty-year-old father. In the winter, they move down to the neighboring

_____ , and stay with relatives.

4. Pocahontas was a(n) _____ when she saved the life of Captain John Smith, in 1613. She was just sixteen. The next year, she married Thomas Rolfe, an English settler. They then visited England, where she died in 1617. She was a(n)

_____ of smallpox.

LESSON   12 (Review) ━━━━◆━━━◆━━━◆━━━◆━

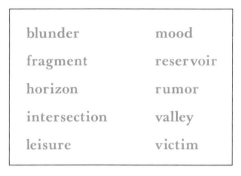

blunder	mood
fragment	reservoir
horizon	rumor
intersection	valley
leisure	victim

A A noun is missing in each sentence below. Find that noun in the above list, and write it in the blank space.

1. Rufus will not have much _____ this week because he has to finish reading a book for a report.

2. Rescuers have reached two of the trapped miners, and they are looking for a third _____ .

3. I had to scrub hard to remove a(n) _____ of food that was stuck to the frying pan.

4. Gladys wanted to drop out of school, but her friends said it would be a(n) _____.

5. The _____ provides our city with excellent drinking water.

6. Traffic was slow at the _____ because the lights were not working properly.

7. One minute she was laughing, and the next she was crying; her _____ changed swiftly.

8. The nearby mountains protect the people who live in the _____ from cold winter winds.

9. An intelligent person should be able to tell the difference between fact and _____.

10. The storm clouds on the _____ are a sign that bad weather is approaching.

52

B One letter is missing in each noun below. Write the missing letter in the space where it belongs. Then write the complete word.

rum __ r	_____	vall __ y	_____
vict __ m	_____	rese __ voir	_____
mo __ d	_____	le __ sure	_____
inte __ section	_____	horiz __ n	_____
fragm __ nt	_____	blund __ r	_____

C Next to each expression below, write a noun that can take its place. Choose your nouns from the above box.

1. place where water is collected and stored   1 _____

2. area of low land between hills   2 _____

3. state of mind   3 _____

4. person injured or killed   4 _____

5. time to do the things you like to do   5 _____

6. part broken off from a whole   6 _____

7. careless or foolish mistake   7 _____

8. unconfirmed report   8 _____

9. place where two or more things cross   9 _____

10. line where the sky seems to meet the earth or the sea   10 _____

D An adjective is needed in each sentence below. Find that adjective in the list at the end of this exercise and write it into the sentence.

1. The crowd was in an angry mood and grew more and more _____ .

2. There was a rumor that some of the Queen's jewels were _____ .

3. The first time I appeared on stage, I made one blunder after another and got myself into a(n) _____ situation.

4. The reservoirs are nearly empty, and water is becoming _____ .

5. I used to be afraid to cross busy intersections, and I am still _____, even when the light is in my favor.

6. You may find life _____ if you have too much leisure.

7. Often, a(n) _____ person is able to spot trouble the instant it appears on the horizon.

8. The victim is _____ whether to bring charges against the thief or remain silent, but she will make her mind up soon.

9. She passed me a note on a fragment of paper, but the message was not _____ , so I could not understand it.

10. The farmers in the neighboring valley are pleased that they have had a(n) _____ supply of rain this spring, but some of the residents in town are not too happy about it.

LIST OF ADJECTIVES (Fill in the two missing letters before moving the adjective up to the sentence where it is needed.)

_ _ ruly	unde _ _ ded
tim _ _	sc _ _ ce
al _ _ t	_ _ gible
_ _ ring	awk _ _ rd
artifi _ _ al	ab _ _ dant

E Consider each question carefully. Then do the following:

1. Next to **Answer**, write "Yes" or "No."

2. Next to **Explanation**, give one or more *good reasons* for your "Yes" or "No."

1. You and another victim are stopped by an armed robber who demands your money. Would you hand over your purse or wallet?

Answer: _____

Explanation: _____

_____

_____

_____

_____

2. It is beginning to snow lightly. On your way to school, you hear a rumor that the school has been closed. Some of your friends decide to return home. Would you make the same decision?

Answer: _____

Explanation: _____

_____

_____

_____

_____

3. You are at an intersection. Traffic is heavy. The light is against you. You see a fairly good chance to run to the other side between the moving cars. Would you take that chance?

Answer: _____

Explanation: _____

_____

_____

_____

_____

F *Listening.* Your teacher will now read an interesting passage to you and give you some questions to answer. Follow your teacher's instructions.

LESSON 13 ━━━━━━━━━━━━

Pronounce each new word. Then write it neatly. Note:

The *a* in **alter** is pronounced *ô*, as in *horn*.

The *c* in **deceive** is pronounced *s*, as in *see*.

alter	ôl′ tər	_____
compensate	käm′ pən sāt	_____
deceive	di sēv′	_____
relish	rel′ ish	_____
select	sə lekt′	_____

Question: What does **compensate** mean in the following sentence?

If you do not have enough money, I will pay the cashier, and you can **compensate** me later.

Answer: The clue to the meaning of **compensate** is an earlier word in the sentence, **pay.** The two words are obviously SYNONYMS. **Compensate** means "pay."

Sometimes the clue to the meaning of a word is a later word:

I will not **alter** my opinion because I have no reason to change it.

Here, we learn the meaning of **alter** from a SYNONYM that comes later in the sentence, **change.**

B Every passage below has a new word like **compensate,** and a SYNONYM of that word, like **pay.** Read carefully and answer the questions.

1. I was asked to choose a topic, but I did not know which one to **select.**

    What does **select** mean? 1 _____

2. We do not **relish** the long trip to the beach, but we enjoy the swimming.

    What does **relish** mean? 2 _____

3. If you mislead us this time, we will not give you a chance to **deceive** us again.

    What does **deceive** mean?   3 _____

4. Everything has changed but you have not **altered.**

    What does **altered** mean?   4 _____

5. The Smiths have been paying their baby-sitters $2.50 an hour, so if they give you less, they will not be **compensating** you fairly.

    What does **compensating** mean?   5 _____

> Note that the new words of this lesson—**alter, compensate, deceive, relish,** and **select**—are *words that express action.* Such words are called *verbs.* The abbreviation for verb is *v.*

 Recognizing Verbs

You can in most cases tell that a word is a verb if you can add *s*, *ing*, and *ed* to its basic form.

For example, **play,** in the sentence "We play baseball," is a verb. Proof: **plays, playing, played.** But **We** is not a verb because you cannot add *s*, *ing*, and *ed* to it. Finally, **baseball** is not a verb because you can add only *s*, but not *ing* and *ed*.

Rules for Adding <u>ING</u> *and* <u>ED</u> *to Verbs*

1. If the verb ends in *e*, drop that *e* before adding *ing* or *ed*.

deceiv~~e~~	+	ing	=	deceiving
deceiv~~e~~	+	ed	=	deceived

2. If the verb does not end in *e*, do not drop any letter.

select	+	ing	=	selecting
select	+	ed	=	selected

Rule for Adding <u>S</u> *to Verbs*

Do not make any change in the verb. Just add the *s*.

deceive	+	s	=	deceives
select	+	s	=	selects

Exceptions: If the verb ends in *s*, *sh*, *ch*, or *x*, put in an *e* before adding *s*.

gues*s*	+	(*e*)	+	s	=	**guesses**
reli*sh*	+	(*e*)	+	s	=	**relishes**
cat*ch*	+	(*e*)	+	s	=	**catches**
rela*x*	+	(*e*)	+	s	=	**relaxes**

Fill in the blank spaces below. The first four answers have been entered as a sample.

1. compensate	+	ing	=	compensating
2. alter	+	ed	=	altered
3. relish	+	s	=	relishes
4. change	+	ed	=	changed
5. relish	+	ing	=	_____
6. alter	+	s	=	_____
7. deceive	+	s	=	_____
8. select	+	ing	=	_____
9. catch	+	s	=	_____
10. mislead	+	ing	=	_____
11. enjoy	+	ed	=	_____
12. alter	+	ing	=	_____
13. deceive	+	ed	=	_____
14. enjoy	+	ing	=	_____
15. relish	+	ed	=	_____
16. choose	+	ing	=	_____
17. pick	+	s	=	_____
18. select	+	ed	=	_____
19. guess	+	s	=	_____
20. relax	+	s	=	_____

Note that some verbs are *irregular*—they do not follow the rules. For example, the verbs **catch, choose, mislead,** and **pay** do not add *ed*, but become **caught, chosen, misled,** and **paid.**

NEW WORD	WHAT IT MEANS	HOW IT IS USED
alter (*v.*) ôl′ tər	make partly but not completely different; change in some way	If my sister buys a dress that is too long, my mother **alters** it by taking up the hem.
	become different; change	Oliver is taller and heavier than he was two years ago, but otherwise he has not **altered**.

TWO YEARS AGO   NOW

NEW WORD	WHAT IT MEANS	HOW IT IS USED
compensate (*v.*) käm′ pən sāt	pay	Some firms pay their employees weekly, and some **compensate** them monthly.
	make amends (make up for injury or loss that one has caused)	Harvey wants to **compensate** for losing his temper. He is willing to apologize.
deceive (*v.*) di sēv′	make (someone) believe what is not true; deal dishonestly with; mislead	Amanda thought that her daughter was attending school, but that was not true. The girl had been **deceiving** her.
	ant. **enlighten**	Let me **enlighten** you about these diamonds. They are artificial. I do not want you to be **deceived**.

relish (v.)	take pleasure in; like;	Harry liked the movie so
rel′ ish	enjoy	much that he would
		relish the opportunity to
		see it again.

I try to do my work right the first time because I do not **relish** the thought of having to do it over.

select (v.)	pick out; choose; take in	A librarian can help you
sə lekt′	preference to others	**select** a book to read in
		your leisure.

I chose chocolate. What flavor did you **select?**

E Which choice makes the sentence correct, *A* or *B?* Write the words of your answer in the blank space.

1. Since Ted borrowed the money from Lisa, _____ will have to be **compensated**.

    A. he   B. she

2. We cannot **select** our _____ .

    A. friends   B. parents

3. You have **altered** so much that your friends are not likely to _____ you.

    A. recognize   B. forget

4. The guests must have **relished** the cake because _____

_____ .

    A. it disappeared very quickly   B. they left it on their plates

5. You **deceived** us by doing _____ you had promised.

    A. no more than   B. the opposite of what

F Read the statements in all the boxes below. Then answer the questions.

Dan was an hour late yesterday. To make up for it, he worked an hour later than usual before going home.

Susan often returned from shopping trips without having bought what she needed because she could not make up her mind.

Ed wanted to change one of his answers after handing in his paper, but he was not allowed to do so.

Marcia had been reluctant to go to the game, but she enjoyed it and is very eager to attend the next one.

Josie was not completely truthful when she told her father that she had no homework.

---

1. Who **deceived** someone?   1 _____

2. Who **compensated** for something?   2 _____

3. Who **relished** something?   3 _____

4. Who had trouble **selecting** things?   4 _____

5. Who could not **alter** something?   5 _____

G *Using Fewer Words.* Replace each italicized expression below with a verb that you studied in this lesson.

1. Do you *take pleasure in* listening to good music?

1 _____

2. I tried to *make up* for my blunder by being especially alert for the rest of the day.

2 _____

3. If you *deal dishonestly with* people, they will soon lose faith in you.

3 _____

4. At the moment, things are the same as they have been, but we expect that they will *change in some way* soon.

4 _____

5. If I need a helper, you are the one I would *take in preference to others*.

5 _____

H Two words are missing in each passage below. Choose those words from the following list and enter them in the blank spaces. Do not use any of these words more than once.

alter	obliging
compensate	offender
enlighten	relish
legible	select

1. I accompanied Mother to the bakery to help her _____ a birthday cake that the whole family would _____ .

2. Cathy wanted to _____ something in the note she was writing to Elwood, but she did not make the change because she was afraid the note might not be _____ .

3. If there is something about the use of the library that you do not understand, ask one of the librarians for help. They will be very glad to _____ you. They are very _____ .

4. During the night, a driver bumped into a light pole on Main Street and damaged it. The _____ , if caught, should be required to _____ the town for the damage.

A Pronounce each new word and write it legibly. Note:

The second *c* in **conceal** is pronounced *s*, as in *see*.

The *s* in **reside** is pronounced *z*, as in *lazy*.

compliment	käm′ plə mənt	_____
conceal	kən sēl′	_____
encounter	in koun′ tər	_____
reside	ri zīd′	_____
respond	ri spänd′	_____

B Read each passage below carefully and answer the question following it.

1. We live in the house on the corner. The Changs **reside** across the street.

   What does **reside** mean? _____

2. Dad had to hide the present from Gina until her birthday. Our neighbors let him **conceal** it in their garage.

   What is the meaning of **conceal**? _____

3. I always congratulate you when you have done well. Did you ever **compliment** me for any of the good things I have done?

   What does **compliment** mean? _____

4. She was given a chance to answer, but she did not **respond.**

   What is the meaning of **respond?** _____

5. Jim was hoping to meet a pedestrian to ask for directions. However, it was past midnight, and he did not **encounter** a living soul.

   What does **encounter** mean? _____

C Fill in the blank spaces below.

1. compliment   +   ing   =   _____

2. congratulate   +   ing   =   _____

3. reside   +   ed   =   _____

4. live   +   ed   =   _____

5. encounter   +   s   =   _____

6. meet   +   ing   =   _____

7. conceal   +   ing   =   _____

8. hide   +   ing   =   _____

9. respond   +   ed   =   _____

10. answer   +   ed   =   _____

11. compliment   +   ed   =   _____

12. reside   +   ing   =   _____

13. encounter   +   ed   =   _____

14. conceal   +   ed   =   _____

15. respond   +   ing   =   _____

16. congratulate   +   ed   =   _____

17. answer   +   ing   =   _____

18. live   +   ing   =   _____

19. reside   +   s   =   _____

20. encounter   +   ing   =   _____

Note that the verbs **hide** and **meet** do not add *ed*, but become **hidden** and **met.** They are *irregular.*

D Study Your New Words

NEW WORD	WHAT IT MEANS	HOW IT IS USED
compliment (v.) käm′ plə mənt	offer a word of praise or admiration to; congratulate	We **complimented** the hostess for her delicious cake.

One classmate **complimented** me on my composition. She said it was very interesting. Another criticized me by saying it was boring.

conceal (v.) kən sēl′	put out of sight; keep secret; hide	Ben Gunn learned where the pirates had **concealed** their treasure.
	ant. **reveal**	When we have good news, we are eager to **reveal** it. When it is bad, we may **conceal** it for a while.
encounter (v.) in koun′ tər	come face to face with; come upon; meet	On the way home I **encountered** a friend of yours. There are supposed to be deer in these woods, but so far we have not **encountered** any.

reside (v.)	live (in or at); have a	Before moving to
ri zīd′	permanent home	Houston, we **resided** in Baltimore.
		In order to vote, people must first register in the district where they **reside.**

respond (v.)	answer; reply; say	Consider the question
ri spänd′	something in return	carefully before you **respond.**
	act as if in answer; react	When the store announces a sale, customers **respond** by buying up almost everything on the counters.

E Which choice makes the sentence correct, *A* or *B?* Write the words of your answer in the blank space.

1. You do not have to indicate where you **reside** if the application form has no blank

   for _____ .

   A. date of birth   B. address

2. The children took turns **concealing** themselves in a game of _____

   _____ .

   A. hide-and-seek   B. follow-the-leader

3. When Sheila scored two baskets in a row, her brother **complimented** her by saying

   _____ .

   A. "Anyone can do that."   B. "Fancy shooting, Sheila."

4. The person who telephoned said she would _____ ,
   so there is no need for you to **respond.**

   A. call again later   B. wait for your call

5. You will probably not **encounter** anyone on _____ .

    A. an uninhabited island   B. Main Street

F   Each set of facts below is followed by a question. Consider the facts carefully before responding.

1. FACTS: At Arlene's house, you wake up in the morning to the cock-a-doodle-doo of the roosters. At Mike's house, the air has a salty tang. At Bruce's house, if you listen, you often hear the sound of airplanes taking off.

    Question: Who resides near the sea?

    Answer: _____

2. FACTS: Lopez hit a home run that tied the game. Evans did not connect with the ball in any of his four times at bat. Rogers made a wild throw that permitted the winning run to score.

    Question: Who deserved to be complimented?

    Answer: _____

3. FACTS: When Millie got home, she found her mother putting together the new kitchen table that had just been delivered, so she helped her. Louise got home early because traffic was light. When Armando got home, he found there was no electricity because of a power failure.

    Question: Who encountered trouble?

    Answer: _____

4. FACTS: Ted has already answered Kaori's invitation. He is coming to her party. Emily has been invited to another party that is to take place the same time as Kaori's, so she is undecided about which invitation to accept. Mindy just called Kaori. She will be delighted to come.

    Question: Who has not responded?

    Answer: _____

5. FACTS: Stan carries his house key on a key ring. Joan can get into her house with her key, which she keeps under the welcome mat. George carries no key because there is always someone home to open the door for him.

    Question: Who conceals something?

    Answer: _____

G *Using Fewer Words.* Replace each italicized expression below with a verb that you studied in this lesson.

1. I looked so bad that I was hoping I would not *come face to face with* anyone I knew.

   1 _____

2. You were the first to *offer a word of praise to* me.

   2 _____

3. Guests were coming, so I rushed to *put out of sight* all the things that were cluttering up my room.

   3 _____

4. We have your summer address, but where do you *have a permanent dwelling*?

   4 _____

5. When someone politely asks you a question, you are expected to *say something in return*.

   5 _____

H Two words are missing in each passage below. Choose those words from the following list and enter them in the blank spaces. Do not use any of these words more than once.

compliment	hearsay
conceal	negligent
encounter	react
familiar	rival

1. There is a rumor that the mayor is trying to _____ some bad news from reporters. People are wondering if this is true, or if it is only

   _____ .

2. We had never been to Jones Beach before, so we were hoping that we might

   _____ someone there that we knew. However, we did not see any-

   one who looked _____ .

3. After winning, I hesitated for a few moments before shaking hands with my

   _____ . I knew she was jealous of me, and I could not tell how she

   would _____ , but she smiled and congratulated me.

4. "I want to _____ you," she said, "for playing a fine game. I made

   several errors. I might have beaten you if I had not been so _____."

alter	encounter
compensate	relish
compliment	reside
conceal	respond
deceive	select

A A verb is missing in each passage below. Find that verb in the above list, and write it in the blank space.

1. On my birthday, Mom and Dad took me to a Chinese restaurant because they know that I

   _____

   Oriental food.

2. The Kaminskys moved about two years ago, but I do not know where they now

   _____.

3. Please make an exact copy. Do not _____ a word.

4. I will reveal the whole truth. I have nothing to _____.

5. When Andy was shopping for a used car, he took along my father's mechanic to

   help him _____ a good one.

6. Pat agreed to baby-sit for the neighbors across the street, and they said they would

   _____ her on their return.

7. If you think you can trust every stranger you _____, you

   are certainly an optimist.

8. Her question puzzled me so much that I did not know how to _____.

9. If you always put your change into your purse or wallet without counting it, you

   are inviting people to _____ you.

10. She received so many congratulations. Several of those who had been in the audi-

    ence came over to _____ her.

B Beside each verb below, write a *synonym* and, if requested, an *antonym*. Choose all your synonyms and antonyms from the Word List at the end of the exercise.

1. **alter** SYN. _____

2. **compensate** SYN. _____

3. **compliment** SYN. _____

4. **conceal** SYN. _____ ANT. _____

5. **deceive** SYN. _____ ANT. _____

6. **encounter** SYN. _____

7. **relish** SYN. _____

8. **reside** SYN. _____

9. **respond** SYN. _____

10. **select** SYN. _____

WORD LIST

change	hide	mislead
choose	like	pay
congratulate	live	reply
enlighten	meet	reveal

C Enter the missing letter or letters in each partly spelled verb below. Then spell the complete verb in the blank at the right. The first answers have been entered as a sample.

1. I do not care for soup but Terry relish__**es**__ it.

1. __**relishes**__

2. It rained, so we alter_____ our plans.

2. _____

3. Why are you deceiv_____ us?

3. _____

4. We have not yet been compensat_____.

4. _____

5. Gina does her own shopping and select_____ her own clothes.

5. _____

6. Do you know where Kent now resid_____?

6. _____

7. Janet is conceal_____ some of the facts.

7. _____

8. Ben smiled when you compliment_____ him.

8. _____

9. You have not respond_____ to my question.

9. _____

10. Are you encounter_____ any problems?

10. _____

D Complete the spelling of the nouns partially spelled. Each blank stands for one missing letter.

1. The salesclerk who gave me the wrong change was not trying to deceive me. I believe it was just a **bl __ __ der** on her part.

2. After the game, the losers came over to compliment the **v __ __ tors.**

3. You were just crying, and now you are laughing. Does your **m __ __ d** always alter so quickly?

4. The guidance counselor helped the **adole __ __ ent** select a foreign language.

5. Let me break off a **fr __ __ ment** of this cookie for you to taste. I am sure you will relish it.

6. The **v __ __ tim** was awarded $500,000 by the court to compensate him for his injuries.

7. More people reside in the **v __ __ leys** than in the hills.

8. As soon as I find some **l __ __ sure,** I will respond to Barry's letter.

9. The **c __ __ prit** took the gems to a friend and asked her to conceal them for him.

10. Jenny is unbeatable. She has yet to encounter a **r __ __ al** who can defeat her.

E Consider each question carefully. Then do the following:

    1. Next to **Answer,** write "Yes" or "No."

    2. Next to **Explanation,** give one or more *good reasons* for your "Yes" or "No."

1. A classmate asks to borrow your notes. You know that this classmate is negligent and may lose your notes, so you tell a lie—that you have lent the notes to somebody else. Is it forgivable to deceive the classmate in this case?

Answer: _____

Explanation: _____

_____

_____

_____

_____

2. You are asked to deliver circulars to the homes in your neighborhood for two hours. However, it takes you more than three hours to do the job. If the employer compensates you for two hours only, would you ask for more money?

Answer: _____

Explanation: _____

_____

_____

_____

_____

_____

3. You have been invited to a party. You later learn that your best friend is not being invited. Would you conceal from your friend the fact that you have received this invitation?

Answer: _____

Explanation: _____

_____

_____

_____

_____

_____

F *Listening.* Your teacher will now read an interesting passage to you and give you some questions to answer. Follow your teacher's instructions.

A Pronounce each new word, noting its spelling. Then write it in the space provided.

benefit	ben′ ə fit	_____
conserve	kən surv′	_____
grieve	grēv	_____
prohibit	prō hib′ it	_____
vanish	van′ ish	_____

B You can learn what the new words mean from the familiar ANTONYMS with which they are used below. Read carefully and answer the questions.

1. Most of our beaches permit swimming, bathing, and surfing, but they **prohibit** fishing.

    (*a*) Which word is an antonym of **prohibit**? _____

    (*b*) What does **prohibit** mean? _____

2. If you waste all your strength in the first moments of the race, you may have to drop out. **Conserve** your energy.

    (*a*) Which word is an antonym of **conserve**? _____

    (*b*) What does **conserve** mean? _____

3. I just saw the moon **vanish** behind a cloud, but it should soon appear again.

    (*a*) Which word is an antonym of **vanish**? _____

    (*b*) What does **vanish** mean? _____

4. After a war, people rejoice that the fighting is over and **grieve** for those who were lost.

    (*a*) Which word is an antonym of **grieve**? _____

    (*b*) What does **grieve** mean? _____

5. Raising the fare may **benefit** the bus company and its employees but harm those passengers who cannot afford the increase.

    (*a*) Which word is an antonym of **benefit**? _____

    (*b*) What does **benefit** mean? _____

C Fill in the blank spaces below.

1. prohibit + ed = _____
2. grieve + s = _____
3. vanish + s = _____
4. benefit + ed = _____
5. conserve + ing = _____
6. grieve + ed = _____
7. prohibit + s = _____
8. vanish + ed = _____
9. benefit + ing = _____
10. conserve + s = _____
11. vanish + ing = _____
12. prohibit + ing = _____
13. conserve + ed = _____
14. grieve + ing = _____
15. benefit + s = _____

D *Study Your New Words*

NEW WORD	WHAT IT MEANS	HOW IT IS USED
benefit (*v.*) ben′ ə fit	do good to or for; help; aid *ant.* **harm**	Rest **benefits** a person who has a cold.
	receive good; be helped; profit	If you have learned something from your past mistakes, you have **benefited** from them.
conserve (*v.*) kən surv′	keep from being used up or wasted; save *ant.* **waste**	One way to **conserve** electricity is to turn off the lights in rooms that are not in use.
		A driver who sits in a parked car with the engine running is **wasting** gasoline, instead of **conserving** it.

grieve (v.) grēv	feel deep grief or sorrow; be sad; mourn *ant.* **rejoice**	The whole town **grieved** for the victims of the crash.
	cause to feel grief; sadden	Our defeat in the championship game **grieves** us, but the victors are **rejoicing**.
prohibit (v.) prō hib′ it	refuse to permit; forbid *ant.* **permit**	The management **prohibits** smoking in certain parts of the theater.

Many motels now **prohibit** pets, but you may be able to find one that **permits** them.

| vanish (v.)
 van′ ish | pass suddenly out of sight; disappear
 ant. **appear** | The moment my back was turned my purse **vanished**. |
| | pass out of existence; cease to exist | The herds of buffalo that used to roam our plains have **vanished**. |

E   Choose the word or expression that makes the sentence correct, and write it in the blank space.

1. Marjorie is **grieving** because her _____ .

    A. best friend is moving to   B. music teacher has complimented
        another state   her

2. I am much better today. I have stopped sneezing, and my _____ has **vanished**.

    A. voice   B. cough

3. In winter, you can **conserve** heating fuel by _____ your room temperature during the night.

    A. lowering   B. raising

4. You cannot _____ across a bridge that **prohibits** pedestrians.

    A. drive   B. walk

5. The improvement in business has not **benefited** those people who are _____

_____ .

    A. getting raises   B. still out of work

F   Read the statements in all the boxes below. Then answer the questions.

> The sudden disappearance of Judge Crater is a mystery that has never been solved.

> After Drew put up his wall shelves, the floor in his room was no longer cluttered with boxes and cartons.

> Barbara was so upset when she lost her dog that she stayed at home and would not go anywhere, even with her friends.

> Felix went into the food business and gave jobs to several people who had been out of work for a long time.

> Marisa had a learner's permit, so she could drive only if accompanied by someone with an operator's license, like Mom or Dad.

1. Who **grieved**?

1 _____

2. Who **vanished**?

2 _____

3. Who was **prohibited** from doing something?

3 _____

4. Who succeeded in **conserving** space?

4 _____

5. Who **benefited** others?

5 _____

G *Using Fewer Words.* Replace each italicized expression below with a verb that you studied in this lesson. Note that some of the required answers are verbs ending in *s, ing,* or *ed*.

1. Once I got to the party, my mood changed, and all my cares *ceased to exist.*

1 _____

2. Dr. Rossi told me to stop taking the medicine because it was not *doing any good for* me.

2 _____

3. Our neighbor *does not permit* ballplaying on his property.

3 _____

4. When water is scarce, we must try to *keep it from being wasted.*

4 _____

5. Most of the fans *felt deep sorrow* over the loss of our best pitcher to another team.

5 _____

LESSON 17 ━━━━━━━━━━━━━━━━

A Pronounce each new word, noting its spelling. Then write it in the space provided.

acknowledge	ək näl′ ij	_____
detest	di test′	_____
display	dis plā′	_____
gratify	grat′ ə fī	_____
harmonize	här′ mə nīz	_____

B You should be able to learn what the new words mean from the familiar ANTONYMS with which they are used below. Read carefully and answer the questions.

1. When you were very young, you must have adored Cinderella and **detested** her cruel stepsisters.

    (*a*) Which word is an antonym of **detested?** _____

    (*b*) What does **detested** mean? _____

2. My friend and I get along well because our opinions usually **harmonize.** Once in a while, though, they clash.

    (*a*) Which word is an antonym of **harmonize?** _____

    (*b*) What does **harmonize** mean? _____

3. Your composition is so superior that it should be **displayed** in the center of the bulletin board, instead of being concealed in a corner.

    (*a*) Which word is an antonym of **displayed?** _____

    (*b*) What does **displayed** mean? _____

4. You will be disappointed to hear that we lost, but you will be **gratified** to know that the team missed you.

    (*a*) Which word is an antonym of **gratified?** _____

    (*b*) What does **gratified** mean? _____

5. At first, the company denied the rumor that it was going out of business, but later it **acknowledged** that the rumor was true.

    (*a*) Which word is an antonym of **acknowledged?** _____

    (*b*) What does **acknowledged** mean? _____

C *Verbs Ending in Y*

Verbs that end in *y*, like **display** and **gratify**, require special attention when we add *ing, ed,* or *s*. Here are the rules.

1. TO ADD <u>ING</u>: Do not change the *y*. Just add *ing*:

$$\text{display} \quad + \text{ing} \quad = \text{displaying}$$
$$\text{gratify} \quad + \text{ing} \quad = \text{gratifying}$$

2. TO ADD <u>ED</u>: First look at the letter before *y* to see if it is a **vowel** or a *consonant*. (*a, e, i, o,* and *u* are *vowels*. All the other letters of the alphabet are **consonants**.)

- If the letter before *y* is a *vowel*, just add *ed:*

display (the letter before *y* is *a,* a vowel) + **ed** = **displayed**

- If the letter before *y* is a *consonant*, change *y* to *i* and add *ed:*

gratif̶y̶ⁱ (the letter before *y* is *f,* a consonant) + **ed** = **gratified**

3. TO ADD <u>S</u>:

- If the letter before *y* is a *vowel*, just add *s:*

display + s = displays

- If the letter before *y* is a *consonant*, do the following:

First change the *y* to *i*.

Then add an *e*.

Then add *s*.

gratif̶y̶ⁱ + (e) + s = gratifies

Important: Be especially alert when you add *ed* or *s* to verbs ending in a *consonant plus y*, like **gratify**.

gratif̶y̶ⁱ + ed = gratified

gratif̶y̶ⁱ + (e) + s = gratifies

Fill in the blank spaces below. The first six blanks have been filled as samples.

1. play + ing = **playing**
2. cry + ing = **crying**
3. delay + ed = **delayed**
4. try + ed = **tried**
5. enjoy + s = **enjoys**
6. deny + s = **denies**
7. gratify + ing = _____
8. delay + ing = _____
9. display + ed = _____
10. reply + ed = _____
11. destroy + s = _____
12. try + s = _____
13. deny + ed = _____
14. enjoy + ed = _____
15. reply + s = _____
16. display + s = _____
17. annoy + ed = _____
18. gratify + ed = _____
19. display + ing = _____
20. gratify + s = _____

D Study Your New Words

NEW WORD	WHAT IT MEANS	HOW IT IS USED
acknowledge (v.) ək näl′ ij	admit the truth or existence of; admit; confess *ant.* **deny** make known that something has been received or noticed	I will gladly **acknowledge** my mistake if you can show me that I am wrong. She **acknowledged** my gift by sending me a thank-you card.

detest (v.) di test′	dislike very much; hate *ant.* **adore**	If you deceive people, they will grow to **detest** you.
		I do not **detest** your brother. I just dislike him.
display (v.) dis plā′	put or spread out to attract attention; put on view; exhibit	The T-shirt I wanted was **displayed** in the store window.
	show; reveal *ant.* **conceal**	Dad **displayed** his annoyance with my sister when he told her not to smoke in the house.
gratify (v.) grat′ ə fī	please; give pleasure to *ant.* **disappoint**	We like to be complimented. A word of praise **gratifies** us and makes us try harder.
	give in to; satisfy	Babies are quick to cry if some of their wishes are not immediately **gratified**.
harmonize (v.) här′ mə nīz	be in *harmony* (agreement); agree; go together in a pleasant way *ant.* **clash**	Tennis shoes are all right with a sports outfit, but they do not **harmonize** with a bridal gown.

| | | |
| bring into harmony or agreement | We are so far apart that it seems impossible to **harmonize** our opinions. |

E Choose the word or expression that makes the sentence correct, and write it in the blank space.

1. I am **gratified** that my name has been _____ the honor roll for the first time.

    A. dropped from   B. added to

2. She **detested** the medicine because it _____.

    A. had a bitter taste   B. made her feel better

3. We bought a _____ refrigerator so that it would **harmonize** with the other brown appliances in our kitchen.

    A. white   B. brown

4. The performer **acknowledged** the applause by _____ .

    A. throwing kisses   B. remaining backstage

5. Many clothing stores are now **displaying** their new styles on _____ .

    A. TV   B. radio

F Each set of facts below is followed by a question. Consider the facts carefully before responding.

1. FACTS: Lori was angry when George, who had just arrived, tried to get ahead of us on the line. But she said nothing. Bill felt the same way, and he finally said, "George, why don't you go to the end of the line where you belong?"

    Question: Who displayed rudeness?

    Answer: _____

2. FACTS: Fran complained that there was no fresh fruit and no cheese. She said that she had not tasted an orange for more than a week, and that French fried potatoes had been served so often that she could no longer look at them.

    Question: What food did Fran detest?

    Answer: _____

3. FACTS: Rudy was declared safe in a close play at home plate. Jason, the catcher, argued with the umpire, insisting that Rudy should have been called out. And Manny, the pitcher, said the same thing.

    Question: Who was probably gratified by the umpire's decision?

    Answer: _____

4. **FACTS:** Terry says sugar is bad for our teeth. She does not eat candy or cake. Nick says we should all be on time, but he is the one who is usually late. Maria says everyone should have a hobby. She likes to go bowling.

    Question: Whose words and actions do not harmonize?

    Answer: _____

5. **FACTS:** I shouted "So long" to Olga, Veronica, and Harry. Olga waved to me, Veronica did not respond, and Harry said, "See you tomorrow."

    Question: Who failed to acknowledge a greeting?

    Answer: _____

G *Using Fewer Words.* Replace each italicized expression below with a verb that you studied in this lesson. Note that some of the required answers may be verbs ending in *s*, *ing*, or *ed*.

1. It *gives pleasure to* parents to know that their children are doing well.

    1 _____

2. When someone sends you a present, you should *make known that you have received* it.

    2 _____

3. The carpeting in your room *goes together in a pleasant way* with the wallpaper and the curtains.

    3 _____

4. Soon, the new automobiles will be *put on view* in showrooms all over the country.

    4 _____

5. I cannot get along with anyone that I *dislike very much.*

    5 _____

LESSON 18 (Review)

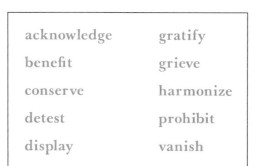

acknowledge	gratify
benefit	grieve
conserve	harmonize
detest	prohibit
display	vanish

A A verb is missing in each passage below. Find that verb in the above list, and write it in the blank space.

1. Dr. Lang says that my injury will leave no permanent scar. All traces of the wound will _____ .

2. I have won the election, but my rival refuses to _____ her defeat.

3. Everyone will _____ if science is successful in its war against disease.

4. It must _____ you to know that your best friend is moving. I am sure you are not happy about it.

5. One way to _____ food is to store leftover meat in the refrigerator and use it the next day in sandwiches.

6. Our traffic regulations _____ speeds of more than 55 miles per hour.

7. She is in favor of having the picnic, and I am against it. On this matter, our ideas do not _____ .

8. Stores invite customers to come in and look around because they cannot _____ all their merchandise in their front windows.

9. Didn't it _____ you to learn that the culprit has been found?

10. What do you think of people who destroy public property and have no respect for the rights of others? I _____ them.

B *Synonyms and Antonyms.* For each italicized verb on line (*a*), enter a SYNONYM on line (*b*) and an ANTONYM on line (*c*). Choose all your synonyms and antonyms from the following list:

acknowledge	conceal	display	permit
adore	conserve	gratify	prohibit
appear	deny	grieve	rejoice
benefit	detest	harm	vanish
clash	disappoint	harmonize	waste

The answers to the first question have been filled in as a sample.

1. (*a*) We must *save* energy.

   (*b*) We must __**conserve**__ energy.

       (Note: **conserve** is a SYNONYM of *save*.)

   (*c*) We must not __**waste**__ energy.

       (Note: **waste** is an ANTONYM of *save*.)

2. (*a*) I *admit* my mistake.

   (*b*) I _____ my mistake.

   (*c*) I do not _____ my mistake.

3. (*a*) The laws *forbid* child labor.

   (*b*) The laws _____ child labor.

   (*c*) The laws do not _____ child labor.

4. (*a*) Our points of view *agree*.

   (*b*) Our points of view _____.

   (*c*) Our points of view do not _____.

5. (*a*) The sun will *disappear* in the West.

   (*b*) The sun will _____ in the West.

   (*c*) In the morning, the sun will _____ in the East.

6. (*a*) We *hate* liars.

   (*b*) We _____ liars.

   (*c*) We do not _____ liars.

7. (a) You have no reason to *mourn*.

 (b) You have no reason to ——————————.

 (c) You have good reason to ——————————.

8. (a) I do not want to *show* my ignorance.

 (b) I do not want to —————————— my ignorance.

 (c) I want to —————————— my ignorance.

9. (a) Peace will *help* everyone.

 (b) Peace will —————————— everyone.

 (c) Peace will —————————— no one.

10. (a) Your answers *please* us.

 (b) Your answers —————————— us.

 (c) Your answers do not —————————— us.

C Enter the missing letter or letters in each partly spelled verb below. Then write the complete verb in the blank at the right. The first answers have been entered as a sample.

1. It griev__es__ me when I see a tree cut down.   1 __grieves__

2. My sneakers have vanish————— .   2 ————————

3. Several famous paintings are being display————— .   3 ————————

4. I benefit————— greatly from my last vacation.   4 ————————

5. Driving without a license is prohibit————— .   5 ————————

6. Are you conserv————— paper?   6 ————————

7. Sue enjoys eating but detest————— washing dishes.   7 ————————

8. Her handbag harmoniz————— with her outfit, but her gloves do not.   8 ————————

9. It is gratify————— to see how you have improved.   9 ————————

10. When I told my cousin Donald that he looked ill, he acknowledg ————— that he had a toothache.   10 ————————

D Complete the spelling of each partly spelled noun by entering the two missing letters.

1. Try to conserve water because the **reserv __ __ rs** are half empty.

2. The host and **hos __ __ ss** were gratified that we came to their dinner.

3. However, they were grieved to hear that one of the **g __ __ sts** who did not come was very ill.

4. Parking near busy **int __ __ sections** is prohibited.

5. The moon has vanished. It just dipped below the **horiz __ __** .

6. Jack is cheerful. He detests **pess __ __ ists**.

7. I am like Jack. I acknowledge that I am an **op __ __ mist**.

8. From the ignorance I displayed about chess, anyone could tell that I was a **nov __ __ e**.

9. The raise that our neighbor has just received will surely benefit him, as well as his **depend __ __ ts**.

10. The driver's description of the accident did not harmonize with the account given by the injured **pedestr __ __ n**.

E Consider each question carefully. Then do the following:

1. Next to **Answer**, write "Yes" or "No."

2. Next to **Explanation**, give one or more *good reasons* for your "Yes" or "No."

1. Your club is planning a picnic. Some of the members want to invite friends as guests, but other members say that the picnic should be for members only. Would you vote to prohibit outsiders?

Answer: _____

Explanation: _____

_____

_____

_____

_____

2. In a softball game, you hit a line drive that smashes a lamp on your neighbor's property. The neighbor is away. When he returns, would you go to him and acknowledge responsibility for the damage?

Answer: _____

Explanation: _____

_____

_____

_____

_____

_____

3. One of the members of the committee to which you have been assigned is a person with whom you have often clashed. Her ideas and yours never seem to harmonize. Would you ask the teacher to assign you to a different committee?

Answer: _____

Explanation: _____

_____

_____

_____

_____

_____

F *Listening.* Your teacher will now read an interesting passage to you and give you some questions to answer. Follow your teacher's instructions.

A Pronounce each new word. Then write it in the space provided. Note:

The *d* in **gradually** is pronounced *j*, as in *joy*.

The *s* in **occasionally** is pronounced *zh*, as in *pleasure*.

considerably	kən sid′ ər ə blē	_____
gradually	graj′ oo wə lē	_____
lately	lāt′ lē	_____
occasionally	ə kā′ zhən ′l ē	_____
seldom	sel′ dəm	_____

B Both sentences in each set below have the same meaning. Read carefully. Then write the meaning of the new word.

1. Ted has improved **considerably.**
   Ted has improved a great deal.

   Considerably means _____.

2. Little by little, the fog disappeared.
   Gradually, the fog disappeared.

   Gradually means _____.

3. Al heard from Emily **lately.**
   Al heard from Emily not long ago.

   Lately means _____.

4. We quarrel once in a while.
   We quarrel **occasionally.**

   Occasionally means _____.

5. She has **seldom** complained.
   She has not often complained.

   Seldom means _____.

> Note that this lesson introduces us to a new kind of word, the *adverb*. **Considerably, gradually, lately, occasionally,** and **seldom** are adverbs. *An adverb modifies (tells about) a verb*. The abbreviation for adverb is *adv*.

C *What Do Adverbs Do?*

An adverb answers such questions as the following:

- *How much,* or *to what extent?*

    Considerably (set 1) is an adverb modifying the verb *has improved*. **Considerably** tells *how much* Ted has improved.

- *How,* or *in what manner?*

    Gradually (set 2) is an adverb modifying the verb *disappeared*. **Gradually** tells *in what manner* the fog disappeared.

- *When,* or *how often?*

    Lately (set 3) is an adverb modifying the verb *heard*. **Lately** tells *when* Al heard from Emily.

Most adverbs end in *ly*. Note, however, that the adverb **seldom** (set 5) does not end in *ly*.

D *Study Your New Words*

NEW WORD	WHAT IT MEANS	HOW IT IS USED
considerably (*adv.*) kən sid′ ər ə blē	a great deal; much	Prices went up **considerably.** You have hardly changed, but your sister has altered **considerably.**

LAST YEAR   NOW

gradually (*adv.*) graj′ oo wə lē	bit by bit; little by little; slowly *ant.* **suddenly**	We did not know each other at first, but we **gradually** became friends. A wound heals **gradually.**
lately (*adv.*) lāt′ lē	not long ago recently	I am familiar with the movie because I saw it **lately.** We used to see Lori almost every day, but we have not encountered her **lately.**
occasionally (*adv.*) ə kā′ zhən ′l ē	once in a while; now and then; sometimes	**Occasionally,** we go to a restaurant for dinner. No one is perfect. Everyone makes a mistake **occasionally.**
seldom (*adv.*) sel′ dəm	not often; rarely; infrequently *ant.* **often**	My friend and I get along very well. We **seldom** disagree. You are very obliging. You **seldom** turn down anyone who asks for a favor.

E Which choice, *A* or *B*, makes the sentence correct? Enter the correct word or words in the blank space.

1. They advanced **gradually,**_____.

    A. one step at a time   B. by leaps and bounds

2. If you are _____ , you will **seldom** get into trouble.

    A. negligent   B. alert

3. We have spaghetti and meatballs **occasionally,** about _____.

    A. three times a week   B. once a month

4. The price used to be $1.09. Now, it is _____, so it has not increased **considerably.**

   A. $1.99   B. $1.19

5. I have had no telephone calls **lately** because all of my friends _____

   _____.

   A. are away on vacation   B. have been calling early in the day

F Read the statements in all the boxes below. Then answer the questions.

> Tony's birthday party was last Friday, and Julia's is next Tuesday. Vera's, you will remember, was just before Thanksgiving, about six months ago.

> Joel made slow but steady progress with his guitar.

> Helen has not missed a single meeting, and neither has Julio, but Cathy came to only two of the ten meetings, and Murray never appeared.

> In the last week, Sandra has moved up from seventh place to second. Emily has slipped from third to fourth. Mona remains in first place.

> Walter was shy and said nothing. Celina, too, had little to say, but once in a while she asked an important question. Dick always had something to say.

1. Who **seldom** attended?   1 _____

2. Who advanced **gradually?**   2 _____

3. Who spoke **occasionally?**   3 _____

4. Who advanced **considerably?**   4 _____

5. Who had a celebration **lately?**   5 _____

G *Using Fewer Words.* Replace each italicized expression below with an adverb that you studied in this lesson.

1. *Bit by bit* I caught up with my rival.   1 _____

2. We visit our relatives *now and then* on holidays.   2 _____

3. There was a serious accident at this intersection *not long ago*.   3 _____

4. *Not often* have we had such fine weather.   4 _____

5. Your sister has changed *a great deal* since we last saw her.   5 _____

LESSON 20

A Pronounce each new word. Then write it in the space provided.

altogether	ôl' tə ge*th*' ər	_____
apparently	ə per' ənt lē	_____
currently	kur' ənt lē	_____
generally	jen' ər ə lē	_____
practically	prak' tik lē	_____

B Both sentences in each set below have the same meaning. Read them carefully. Then write the meaning of the new word.

1. Children are **generally** impatient.
   Children are usually impatient.

    Generally means _____.

2. At the present time lettuce is scarce.
   Currently lettuce is scarce.

    Currently means _____.

3. Frank was **altogether** right.
   Frank was completely right.

    Altogether means _____.

4. Carmela's skates are almost new.
   Carmela's skates are **practically** new.

    Practically means _____.

5. The rumor, as far as one can see, is true.
   The rumor, **apparently,** is true.

    Apparently means _____.

C What Do Adverbs Do?

In our last lesson we learned that an adverb modifies a *verb*. For example, in

We quarrel occasionally,

the adverb **occasionally** modifies the verb *quarrel*. **Occasionally** tells *when* we quarrel.

In our present lesson, we see that an adverb may sometimes modify an *adjective:*

Generally (set 1) is an adverb modifying the adjective *impatient*.

Generally tells *how often* children are impatient.

Currently (set 2) is an adverb modifying the adjective *scarce*.

Currently tells *when* lettuce is scarce.

Altogether (set 3) is an adverb modifying the adjective *right*.

Altogether tells *to what extent* Frank was right.

> An adverb may modify an adjective, as well as a verb.

D Study Your New Words

NEW WORD	WHAT IT MEANS	HOW IT IS USED
altogether (*adv.*) ôl′ tə ge*th*′ ər	completely; wholly	Her excuse for coming late was **altogether** incredible.
	on the whole; considering everything	We won five games and lost two. **Altogether,** it was a good season.
apparently (*adv.*) ə per′ ənt lē	obviously; evidently; as far as one can see	It was past midnight. All the lights in the house were out. Everyone was **apparently** asleep.
		Dad could not start the car. Something was **apparently** wrong with the battery.

currently (*adv.*) kur′ ənt lē	at the present time; now	The pen you bought last week for $2.95 is **currently** selling for $1.95. Alton is **currently** popular because he scored the winning goal in last week's game.
generally (*adv.*) jen′ ər ə lē	usually; in most cases; as a rule	Traffic is **generally** heavy on Main Street in the late afternoon. I am surprised that Ginny is not here yet because she **generally** gets home before me.
practically (*adv.*) prak′ tik lē	almost; nearly; to all intents and purposes	At five in the morning, the streets are **practically** deserted. It has almost stopped raining. The storm is **practically** over.

E Which choice, *A* or *B*, makes the sentence correct? Enter the correct word or words in the blank space.

1. The stranger wore _____ . He was **apparently** wealthy.

   A. dark glasses   B. expensive clothes

2. Katsuko is running for president. She _____ **currently** our treasurer.

   A. is   B. was

3. Lenny has been playing the recorder for about _____ . He is **practically** a novice.

   A. four years   B. three weeks

4. You are supposed to report at nine. If you arrive after nine about _____

   _____ , you are **generally** late.

   A. four times a week   B. twice a month

5. To _____ , the future looks **altogether** hopeless.

    A. an intelligent person   B. a pessimist

F Read each passage and answer the questions.

Anne, Charley, and Roger were on a checkout line that was hardly moving. Charley was reading an article in a sports magazine. After ten minutes, Anne said, "I don't know whether to stay or go to another store." Roger said he was sure that the line would soon start moving quickly.

    Question 1:   Who was apparently an optimist?

    Answer: _____

    Question 2:   Who seemed altogether at ease?

    Answer: _____

The Rovers won, 2-0. Antonelli hit a pair of home runs and did the pitching. The regular catcher, Haskins, is still nursing a broken wrist, so Martinez did the catching. Washburn made an error, his first in two years. Carter swung too quickly at slow balls and struck out three times.

    Question 3:   Who is generally reliable?

    Answer: _____

    Question 4:   Who practically won the game for the Rovers?

    Answer: _____

    Question 5:   Who is currently recovering?

    Answer: _____

G *Using Fewer Words.* Replace each italicized expression below with an adverb that you studied in this lesson.

1. *As a rule* our mail is delivered before noon.

   1 _____

2. There are just four slices left. We are *to all intents and purposes* out of bread.

   2 _____

3. *At the present time* we do not owe a cent to anyone.

   3 _____

4. Traffic is at a standstill. *As far as one can see* there has been an accident.

   4 _____

5. There was a bit of sun in the morning, and almost none in the afternoon. *On the whole* it has been a cloudy day.

   5 _____

H Two words are missing in each passage below. Choose those words from the following list and enter them in the blank spaces. Do not use any of these words more than once.

altogether	generally
deny	practically
display	reservoir
evidently	victim

1. We had a water shortage last summer. The town _____ was almost empty. Now it is _____ full. It cannot hold much more water.

2. Elliott lost his temper. We were all surprised because he is_____ able to control himself. We had never seen him _____ any anger.

3. I _____ the charges that my opponent in this election is making against me. They are _____ false. There is not one word of truth in them.

4. A police car and an ambulance were blocking the intersection of Graham Avenue and Tenth Street. _____ , a pedestrian had been hurt. We could not learn the name of the _____ .

altogether	gradually
apparently	lately
considerably	occasionally
currently	practically
generally	seldom

A An adverb is missing in each passage below. Find that adverb in the above list, and write it in the blank space.

1. I had worn the shoes only once. They were _____ new.

2. As night approaches, the sky _____ becomes darker.

3. She used to ride her bicycle quite often, but now she _____ uses it.

4. No one is right all the time. Even an expert makes a mistake _____ .

5. _____ my sister has not left for work yet. Her car is still on the driveway.

6. Many stores are _____ running sales, so now is a good time to shop.

7. There is not one word of truth in that rumor. It is _____ untrue.

8. I am almost sure we will see Pat today because she _____ has lunch with us.

9. Drew is fourteen, and his sister is _____ younger. She is five.

10. We had some heavy rainstorms about five weeks ago, but it has not rained much _____ .

B *Turning Adjectives Into Adverbs*

Many adjectives become adverbs by adding **ly**.

ADJECTIVE   +   LY   =   ADVERB

negligent   +   ly   =   negligently

Change the following adjectives to adverbs:

1. timid   +   ly   =   _____
2. awkward   +   ly   =   _____
3. artificial   +   ly   =   _____
4. scarce   +   ly   =   _____
5. abundant   +   ly   =   _____
6. permanent   +   ly   =   _____
7. familiar   +   ly   =   _____
8. reluctant   +   ly   =   _____
9. obliging   +   ly   =   _____
10. impatient   +   ly   =   _____

Exception: If the adjective ends in **ble,** drop the **e** and add only **y:**

incredible − e + y = incredibly

THE BALLOON REACHED
AN INCREDIBLE HEIGHT.

11. legible   −   e   +   y   =   _____
12. possible   −   e   +   y   =   _____
13. probable   −   e   +   y   =   _____
14. capable   −   e   +   y   =   _____
15. considerable −   e   +   y   =   _____

C *Turning Adverbs Into Adjectives*

Many adverbs can become adjectives by dropping **ly.**

ADVERB	−	LY	=	ADJECTIVE
gradually	−	**ly**	=	**gradual**

THE SUN IS GRADUALLY
MELTING THE ICE.

Change the following adverbs to adjectives:

1. apparently − ly = _____
2. practically − ly = _____
3. generally − ly = _____
4. occasionally − ly = _____
5. currently − ly = _____
6. dangerously − ly = _____
7. fortunately − ly = _____
8. normally − ly = _____
9. accidentally − ly = _____
10. usually − ly = _____

Exception: If the adverb ends in **bly,** drop the **y** and add only **e:**

incredibly − y + e = incredible

11. considerably − y + e = _____
12. possibly − y + e = _____
13. legibly − y + e = _____
14. probably − y + e = _____
15. capably − y + e = _____

D *Using Adjectives and Adverbs*

We can often express an idea by using either an adjective or an adverb:

Why were you so __**impatient**__?
ADJ.

OR

Why did you act so __**impatiently**__?
ADV.

One word—either an adjective or an adverb— is missing in each second sentence below. Fill in the missing word. The first two answers have been entered as samples.

1. As a beginner, I was an awkward skater.

   As a beginner, I skated __**awkwardly**__ .

2. You came to the party reluctantly.

   You were a __**reluctant**__ guest.

3. Some new pupils are timid.

   Some new pupils behave _____ .

4. We have an abundant supply of stamps.

   We are _____ supplied with stamps.

5. Everyone can make a mistake occasionally.

   Everyone can make an _____ mistake.

6. Your handwriting is legible.

   You write _____ .

7. Who is currently the champion?

   Who is the _____ champion?

8. Her luck was incredible.

   She was _____ lucky.

E Consider each question carefully. Then do the following:

1. Next to **Answer,** write "Yes" or "No."

2. Next to **Explanation,** write one or more *good reasons* for your "Yes" or "No."

1. Lately, Jill has had an occasional toothache, but each time the pain has gone away by itself. For this reason she thinks that she does not have to go to the dentist. Is she making the right decision?

Answer: _____

Explanation: _____

_____

_____

_____

_____

2. You have a chance to play tennis, or checkers, or some other game, against a player who is considerably superior to you. Could you benefit in any way by playing against this rival?

Answer: _____

Explanation: _____

_____

_____

_____

_____

3. An expensive camera that some of your friends already own is currently on sale for half price. You are eager to buy it. But your sister points out that you seldom take pictures and that you can borrow her camera whenever you want to. She advises you to spend your money on something else. Would you take her advice?

Answer: _____

Explanation: _____

_____

_____

_____

_____

F *Listening.* Your teacher will now read an interesting passage to you and give you some questions to answer. Follow your teacher's instructions.

LESSON 22 ━━━━━━━━━━━━━

A Pronounce each new word. Then write it in the space provided. Note:

The *g* in **generous** is pronounced *j*, as in *joy*.

The *g* in **privilege**, too, has the sound of *j*, as in *joy*.

annually	an′ yoo wəl ē	_____
generous	jen′ ər əs	_____
imitate	im′ ə tāt	_____
popular	päp′ yə lər	_____
privilege	priv′ ′l ij	_____

B Both sentences in each set below have the same meaning. Read carefully. Then write the meaning of the new word.

1. Most clubs elect new officers once a year.
   Most clubs elect new officers **annually**.

   Annually means _____.

2. Not everyone is willing to share with others.
   Not everyone is **generous**.

   Generous means _____.

3. The people we admire are the ones we try to be like.
   The people we admire are the ones we **imitate**.

   Imitate means _____.

4. Anne is very well liked.
   Anne is **popular**.

   Popular means _____.

5. The President has the special right of living in the White House.
   The President has the **privilege** of living in the White House.

   Privilege means _____.

C Study Your New Words

NEW WORD	WHAT IT MEANS	HOW IT IS USED
annually (adv.) an′ yoo wəl ē	each year; yearly	To rent a garage, some people pay $50 a month, or $600 **annually**.
	once a year	The law requires drivers to have their cars inspected **annually**.
generous (adj.) jen′ ər əs	willing to share with others; unselfish *ant.* **stingy**	Our **generous** neighbors told us that we are welcome to swim in their backyard pool.
	large; plentiful	For dessert, I was served a **generous** slice of watermelon.
imitate (v.) im′ ə tāt	try to be like or act like; copy	Younger children **imitate** their older brothers and sisters.
	act like, in fun; mimic	Dalma got a great deal of applause when she **imitated** some famous comedy stars.
popular (adj.) päp′ yə lər	very well liked; having many friends and acquaintances	Marty is sure to be elected if he runs because he is one of our most **popular** members.
	liked by most people	Corned beef and cabbage is a **popular** dish.
privilege (n.) priv′ ′l ij	special right	Membership in the public library gives you the **privilege** of borrowing books without charge.
		At 18, an American citizen has the **privilege** of voting in federal, state, and local elections.

D Which choice, *A* or *B*, makes the sentence correct? Enter the correct word or words in the blank space.

1. You cannot truthfully say that your teeth are examined **annually** if your last visit to the dentist was _____ ago.

    A. two years   B. eight months

2. My brother works in the supermarket, so he has the **privilege** of buying our food at _____ prices.

    A. regular   B. reduced

3. We generally do not **imitate** someone that we _____ .

    A. detest   B. adore

4. When I offered Howie some peanuts, he took such a **generous** helping that there was _____ left for me.

    A. more than enough   B. hardly anything

5. If you are going to a very **popular** show or sports event, you should buy your tickets _____ of the performance.

    A. the night   B. in advance

E Read the statements in all the boxes below. Then answer the questions.

Angela told her brother Stanley that he was free to use her computer whenever she was not using it.

Peter went into the lemonade business after he learned that Jenny had earned $30 selling lemonade.	In the election for class president, Bruce got 16 votes, Mary Ann 10, and Geraldine 2. The teacher conducted the election.

Harriet used to spend the July 4 weekend visiting Aunt Mary.

When Drew needed a paper clip, he asked Adrienne if he could borrow one from her, since she had an abundant supply, but she said she could not spare any.

1. Who was apparently not **generous?**   1 _____

2. Who **imitated** someone?   2 _____

3. Who received a **privilege?**   3 _____

4. Who did something **annually?**   4 _____

5. Who seemed not too **popular?**   5 _____

F *Using Fewer Words.* Replace each italicized expression below with a word that you studied in this lesson.

1. Even though you are the captain, you must obey the rules. You do not have the *special right* of doing as you please.   1 _____

2. Paul has set a bad example, so it would be a mistake to *try to act like* him.   2 _____

3. About how much does it cost your brother *each year* for automobile insurance?   3 _____

4. Sports are *liked by most people* in this town.   4 _____

5. The only thing wrong with you is that you are occasionally not too *willing to share with others.*   5 _____

I WAS SERVED A GENEROUS SLICE.

LESSON 23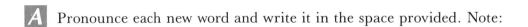

A Pronounce each new word and write it in the space provided. Note:

The *s* in **hesitate** is pronounced *z*, as in *zero*.

hesitate	hez′ ə tāt	_____
hobby	häb′ ē	_____
occupation	äk′ yə pā′ shən	_____
otherwise	u*th*′ ər wīz	_____
principal	prin′ sə pəl	_____

B Both sentences in each set below have the same meaning. Read carefully. Then write the meaning of the new word.

1. There is just one ticket left. Someone else will buy it if you fail to act promptly.
   There is just one ticket left. Someone else will buy it if you **hesitate.**

   Hesitate means _____.

2. Do you have a spare-time activity that you like to work at?
   Do you have a **hobby?**

   Hobby means _____.

3. What is your uncle's line of work?
   What is your uncle's **occupation?**

   Occupation means _____.

4. The soup was a bit salty, but in all other ways the meal was excellent.
   The soup was a bit salty, but **otherwise** the meal was excellent.

   Otherwise means _____.

5. What was your most important reason for changing your mind?
   What was your **principal** reason for changing your mind?

   Principal means _____.

6. Mrs. Collins is the head of the school.
   Mrs. Collins is the **principal.**

   Principal means _____.

C Study Your New Words

NEW WORD	WHAT IT MEANS	HOW IT IS USED
hesitate (v.) hez′ ə tāt	wait or stop for a moment; fail to act promptly; pause	If I am offered a good part in the play, I will not **hesitate.** I will accept it immediately. The house could have burned to the ground if the owner had **hesitated** in calling the fire department.
hobby (n.) häb′ ē	spare-time activity that one likes to do or work at; pastime	Our dentist's **hobby** is playing the piano. Farmers raise vegetables for a living, but we grow them as a **hobby.**
occupation (n.) äk′ yə pā′ shən	work that a person does to earn a living; line of work; trade, business, or profession	Dan wants to be a firefighter. What **occupation** would you like to go into? Lola is a computer programmer, and her brother, too, is preparing for that **occupation.**
otherwise (adv.) u*th*′ ər wīz	in all other ways if things were different	It was cloudy in the morning, but **otherwise** it was a pleasant day. Pearl was ill. **Otherwise** she would have come to the meeting.
principal (adj.) prin′ sə pəl	most important; main; chief	One of the **principal** things to do when you have a cold is to get plenty of rest.
(n.)	head of a school	If you do superior work, you will get a certificate of merit from the **principal.**

IMPORTANT: Note that **principal** can be used either as a *noun* (n.) or an *adjective* (adj.).

D Which choice, *A* or *B*, makes the sentence correct? Enter the correct word or words in the blank space.

1. The **principal** part in a play is seldom given to a _____ .

    A. novice   B. star

2. We know a mechanic who _____ as a **hobby.**

    A. raises pigeons   B. tunes engines

3. I overslept. **Otherwise** I would have been _____ .

    A. on time   B. late

4. Ralph is a barber, and Belle is in a similar **occupation.** She is a _____ .

    A. housewife   B. beautician

5. Generally, people who are _____ do not **hesitate.**

    A. undecided   B. impatient

E Each set of facts below is followed by one or more questions. Consider the facts carefully before responding.

FACTS: Ruth put on one of her magic shows at Steve's party. Cheryl and George helped her. George used to do magic tricks himself, but that was a long time ago.

Question 1: Who was the principal performer?

Answer: _____

Question 2: Who has apparently given up a hobby?

Answer: _____

FACTS: When the fire gong sounded, Dennis rushed out of the building. Judy followed. Cora thought it might be a false alarm, so she did nothing until she smelled smoke.

Question 3: Who hesitated?

Answer: _____

FACTS: Reggie sent back the mashed potatoes because he had ordered French fries. Billie thought of sending back her salad because it had a dressing that she had not asked for. Since she was hungry, she ate the salad, and it was delicious. Angie liked her fish sandwich.

Question 4: Who had one complaint but was otherwise satisfied?

Answer: _____

FACTS: When the department store went out of business, Marian, Nina, and Ernie lost their jobs as checkout clerks. Nina immediately got a similar job in another store. Marian went to secretarial school and later found a job as a typist. Ernie is still looking for work.

Question 5:   Who went into a new occupation?

Answer: _____

F   *Using Fewer Words.* Replace each italicized expression below with a word that you studied in this lesson.

1. What *line of work* is your neighbor in?   1 _____

2. Our teacher says it is often advisable to *stop for a moment* before responding.   2 _____

3. Her *most important* suggestion is that we should check carefully before writing the answers.   3 _____

4. Do you have a(n) *spare-time activity that you like to work at?*   4 _____

5. Vincent was at home because his grandparents were visiting. *If things were different*, he would have been at the game with us.   5 _____

6. The *head of the school* visited our class to listen to some of our compositions.   6 _____

OCCUPATION: CHEF

LESSON 24 (Review)

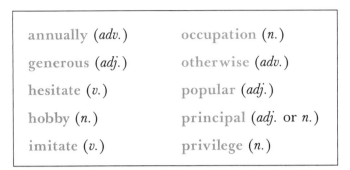

annually (*adv.*)	occupation (*n.*)
generous (*adj.*)	otherwise (*adv.*)
hesitate (*v.*)	popular (*adj.*)
hobby (*n.*)	principal (*adj.* or *n.*)
imitate (*v.*)	privilege (*n.*)

A A word is missing in each passage below. Find that word in the above box, and write it in the blank space.

1. Who does not like ice cream? It is one of our most _____ desserts.

2. As soon as you hit the ball, run to first as fast as you can. Do not _____.

3. Cindy no longer collects stamps. She has outgrown that _____.

4. If you buy something in this store, you have the _____ of returning it within five days for an exchange or a refund.

5. Stanley deserves a bit of the blame, but you are the _____culprit.

6. The farmer could not make a living from his _____ , so he went into another line of work.

7. Zelda got off to a bad start. _____ she would have won.

8. There is no need to buy paper napkins because we still have a(n) _____ supply.

9. Brian said he could bark like a dog and meow like a cat, so I asked if he could _____ a lion.

10. Dr. Blake is the head of our school. Who is your _____ ?

11. An employee who is paid $1000 a month earns $12,000 _____ .

B Complete the following:

1. hesitate   +   ing   =   _____

2. generous   +   ly   =   _____

3. imitate   +   ed   =   _____

4. annually   −   ly   =   _____

5. hesitated   −   ed   =   _____

6. popular   +   ly   =   _____

7. imitating   −   ing   =   _____

8. principal   +   ly   =   _____

9. hesitate   +   s   =   _____

10. considerably −   ly   =   _____

C In each set below, make sentence (b) similar in meaning to sentence (a) by adding a word to sentence (b). Choose all your words from the box on page 112. You may add or drop **ly, ed, ing,** or **s,** if necessary.

The first answer has been entered as a sample.

1. (a) She paused before answering the question.

   (b) She __**hesitated**__ before answering the question.

2. (a) They have always treated us unselfishly.

   (b) They have always been _____ to us.

3. (a) The visiting team has the special right of batting first.

   (b) The visiting team has the _____ of batting first.

4. (a) How much does your sister earn yearly?

   (b) What is your sister's _____ salary?

5. (a) She always mimics me.

   (b) She always _____ me.

6. (a) What is your main interest?

   (b) What are you _____ interested in?

7. (*a*) I used to collect seashells as a pastime.

(*b*) Collecting seashells used to be a(n) ＿＿＿＿＿＿＿＿＿ of mine.

8. (*a*) I have not been copying anyone.

(*b*) I have not been ＿＿＿＿＿＿＿＿＿ anyone.

9. (*a*) What was your grandfather's trade?

(*b*) What was your grandfather's ＿＿＿＿＿＿＿＿ ?

10. (*a*) Oscar has many friends and acquaintances.

(*b*) Oscar is ＿＿＿＿＿＿＿＿ .

D Consider each question carefully. Then do the following:

1. Next to **Answer,** write "Yes" or "No."

2. Next to **Explanation,** write one or more good reasons for your "Yes" or "No."

1. Your team is losing, principally because of careless playing. Several of your teammates have started to blame the umpire. You believe that the umpire has been very fair. Would you say what you believe, even though it might make you less popular?

Answer: ＿＿＿＿

Explanation: ＿＿＿＿＿＿＿＿＿＿＿＿＿＿＿＿＿＿＿＿＿＿＿＿＿＿

＿＿＿＿＿＿＿＿＿＿＿＿＿＿＿＿＿＿＿＿＿＿＿＿＿＿＿＿＿＿＿＿

＿＿＿＿＿＿＿＿＿＿＿＿＿＿＿＿＿＿＿＿＿＿＿＿＿＿＿＿＿＿＿＿

＿＿＿＿＿＿＿＿＿＿＿＿＿＿＿＿＿＿＿＿＿＿＿＿＿＿＿＿＿＿＿＿

＿＿＿＿＿＿＿＿＿＿＿＿＿＿＿＿＿＿＿＿＿＿＿＿＿＿＿＿＿＿＿＿

2. Lately, you have been leaving for school practically half asleep, and you have not been finishing your homework. For this reason, your mother is thinking of taking away your privilege of watching TV after dinner. Is this the best way to deal with the problem?

Answer: _____

Explanation: _____

_____

_____

_____

_____

_____

3. You have a friend who generally does what you do. If you choose a topic, your friend chooses the same one. If you take up a hobby, your friend takes it up, too. Would you ask this friend to stop imitating you?

Answer: _____

Explanation: _____

_____

_____

_____

_____

_____

E *Listening.* Your teacher will now read an interesting passage to you and give you some questions to answer. Follow your teacher's instructions.

LESSON 25

A Pronounce each new word and write it in the space provided. Note:

The *ci* in **depreciate** is pronounced *shē*, as in *she*.

The *sc* in **descend** is pronounced *s*, as in *sell*.

demolish	di mäl′ ish	_____
demote	di mōt′	_____
depreciate	di prē′ shē āt	_____
depress	di pres′	_____
descend	di send′	_____

B Both sentences in each set below have the same meaning. Read carefully. Then write the meaning of the new word.

1. The building is being torn down.
   The building is being **demolished.**

   Demolished means_____.

2. The director was moved down in rank to assistant director.
   The director was **demoted** to assistant director.

   Demoted means_____.

3. A new computer goes down in value considerably the first year you own it.
   A new computer **depreciates** considerably the first year you own it.

   Depreciates means_____.

4. The bell will not ring if you press down the button lightly.
   The bell will not ring if you **depress** the button lightly.

   Depress means_____.

5. Watch your step as you move down the ladder.
   Watch your step as you **descend** the ladder.

   Descend means_____.

PREFIXES. All the new words in this lesson begin with the prefix **de**, meaning "down." A *prefix* is *a sound added to the beginning of a word to form a new word*. Examples:

PREFIX	+ WORD	= NEW WORD
un ("not")	+ **true**	= **untrue** ("not true")
de ("down")	+ **press**	= **depress** ("press down")

Sometimes the prefix is added to a *root* (a part of a word used to form other words):

de ("down")	+ **scend** (a root meaning "climb")	= **descend** ("climb down")

Remember that the prefix **de** means "down."

C Study Your New Words

NEW WORD	WHAT IT MEANS	HOW IT IS USED
demolish (*v.*) di mäl′ ish	tear down; raze; smash; destroy *ant.* **construct; build**	A reckless driver crashed into our wooden fence and **demolished** it. Several homes built only a few years ago are being **demolished** to make way for the new expressway.
demote (*v.*) di mōt′	reduce or move down to a lower grade or rank *ant.* **promote**	The manager was **demoted** and is now serving as the coach. If you do well, you will be **promoted,** and if you do not, you may be **demoted,** or even dismissed.

depreciate (*v.*) di prē′ shē āt	go down in value or price *ant.* **appreciate**	The new car that Dad bought recently has **depreciated.** It is worth less now. But a 50-year-old car that sold for a few hundred dollars when it was new is now worth thousands because it is an antique. It has **appreciated.**
	make seem unimportant; belittle	She has a good record, but she calls herself a failure. She is always **depreciating** herself.
depress (*v.*) di pres′	press down	When you are learning to play the guitar, it may hurt your fingers at first as you **depress** the strings.
	make gloomy or sad; discourage; sadden	We lost 7-0. The defeat **depressed** us.

descend (*v.*) di send′	move down from a higher to a lower place; go down; climb down	Hold on to the banister as you **descend** the staircase.
	ant. **ascend; climb**	We **ascended** the mountain on Thursday morning and **descended** the following afternoon.

SUFFIXES. A *suffix* is *a sound added to the end of a word.*
We are already familar with the following suffixes:
ed, ing, s, and **ly.**

D Write the words that we get when we add the suffixes indicated below.

1. discourage + ing = _____
2. depreciate + s = _____
3. descend + ed = _____
4. demote + ing = _____
5. impatient + ly = _____
6. belittle + ing = _____
7. demolish + s = _____
8. depreciate + ed = _____
9. raze + ing = _____
10. legible + ly = _____
11. depress + s = _____
12. promote + ed = _____
13. climb + s = _____
14. sadden + ed = _____
15. permanent + ly = _____
16. incredible + ly = _____
17. depreciate + ing = _____
18. ascend + ing = _____
19. undecided + ly = _____
20. entertain + ed = _____

THE ELEPHANTS _____ US YESTERDAY.

E Which choice, *A* or *B*, makes the sentence correct? Enter the correct word or words in the blank space.

1. My camera is now worth _____ than I paid for it. It has **depreciated.**

    A. less   B. more

2. In the closing moments, one of our players _____, and that **demolished** our hopes of victory.

    A. scored a goal   B. fumbled a pass

3. It would certainly _____ me if I were **demoted.**

    A. grieve   B. gratify

4. A pedestrian generally finds it _____ to **ascend** a hill than to descend it.

    A. harder   B. easier

5. _____ usually **depress** us.

    A. Pessimists   B. Optimists

F Read the statements in all the boxes below. Then answer the questions.

> When Ellen dropped the ball, Geri called her "Butterfingers." Ellen, naturally, felt sad.

> The old barn was falling apart, so Ezra knocked it down with his bulldozer. His neighbor Harley, who had just built a new garage, was delighted that he would no longer have to look at the old barn.

> After two months as office manager, Angela asked to have her old job as book-keeper back, and her request was granted. That is how Stanley, the new book-keeper, became the office manager.

> Bruce took the elevator to the third floor and met Sue, who was waiting for the down elevator. When it did not come right away, she grew impatient and took the stairs.

1. Who was **promoted**?   1 _____

2. Who **constructed** something? 2 _____

3. Who was **depressed**?   3 _____

4. Who **descended**?   4 _____

5. Who **demolished** something?   5 _____

6. Who **belittled** somebody?   6 _____

7. Who was **demoted**?   7 _____

8. Who **ascended**?   8 _____

G *Using Fewer Words.*   Replace each italicized expression below with a word that you studied in this lesson.

1. Divers *go down* into deep water to fish for pearls.   1 _____

2. Blake will resign if the new owners *reduce* him *to a lower rank*.   2 _____

3. Your rival obviously does not like you because she always tries to *make* you *seem unimportant*.   3 _____

4. A tornado will swiftly *tear down* anything that stands in its path.   4 _____

5. I knew I would *make* you *gloomy* if I told you the bad news.   5 _____

LESSON 26 ━━━━━━━━━━━━━━━━

A Pronounce each new word and write it in the blank space. Note:

The first syllable of **renovate** is pronounced *ren*.

In all the other new words below, the first syllable is pronounced *ri*, as in *remind*.

recall	ri kôl′	_____
recover	ri kuv′ ər	_____
renovate	ren′ ə vāt	_____
resume	ri zōōm′	_____
revive	ri vīv′	_____

B Both sentences in each set below have the same meaning. Read carefully. Then write the meaning of the new word.

1. I tried to call back to mind exactly what you said yesterday.
   I tried to **recall** exactly what you said yesterday.

   Recall means_____.

2. Pam lost the ball, but she was able to get it back.
   Pam lost the ball, but she was able to **recover** it.

   Recover means_____.

3. We will make the kitchen new again by replacing the old stove, refrigerator, and sink with up-to-date equipment.
   We will **renovate** the kitchen by replacing the old stove, refrigerator, and sink with up-to-date equipment.

   Renovate means_____.

4. Work comes to a halt at lunchtime and begins again about an hour later.
   Work comes to a halt at lunchtime and **resumes** about an hour later.

   Resumes means_____.

5. The lifeguards were able to bring the half-drowned victim back to consciousness.
   The lifeguards were able to **revive** the half-drowned victim.

   Revive means_____.

> **RE:** The prefix **re** means "back" or "again."
>
> **re** ("back") + **call**   = **recall** ("call back")
>
> **re** ("again") + **capture** = **recapture** ("capture again")

C Study Your New Words

NEW WORD	WHAT IT MEANS	HOW IT IS USED
recall (*v.*) ri kôl′	call back to mind; remember *ant.* **forget**	I was not able to open the lock because I could not **recall** the combination.
	call back; cause to return; order back	Last January, the company dismissed four workers. But it has just **recalled** them because business has improved.
recover (*v.*) ri kuv′ ər	get back; regain	Watch your belongings. If they are stolen, you are not likely to **recover** them.
	get well again	You have not completely **recovered** because you still cough a bit.
renovate (*v.*) ren′ ə vāt	make new again, or like new; restore to good condition	It is generally cheaper to **renovate** an old house than to demolish it and build a new one.
		The house has been **renovated** with a new roof and new siding. It looks as if it were just built.
resume (*v.*) ri zoom′	begin again	The rain stopped for a while, but soon it **resumed**.
	take again; occupy again	I got up to open a window, and then I **resumed** my seat.

revive (v.)
ri vīv′

bring back to life or consciousness; make strong again

The plant looked dead when she brought it home, but she was able to **revive** it.

come back to life; become strong or fresh again

As soon as the plant was given some water, it **revived**.

D Complete each sentence below by filling in the *s*, *ing*, or *ed* form of one of the following verbs:

recall   recover   renovate   resume   revive

SAMPLE: Terry ___**recalls**___ faces easily, but she forgets names.

1. Walter is _____ from a sprained ankle.

2. Our town is _____ some of the roads that are in poor condition.

3. My sister had given up cigarettes, but lately she has _____ smoking.

4. Divers are _____ some of the cargo from the sunken freighter.

5. Two witnesses were _____ for further questioning.

6. We were very depressed until the cheerleaders _____ our dying hopes.

7. The pain stops for a few hours. Then it _____ .

8. The birds are coming back, and the trees that seemed to have no life in them are slowly _____ .

9. I take a long time to get over a cold, but Steve _____ quickly.

10. The old place looks like new. It has been completely _____ .

BEFORE   AFTER

E Which choice, *A* or *B*, makes the sentence correct? Write the correct word or words in the blank space.

1. You must have a _____ memory because you **recall** easily.

    A. good   B. poor

2. The war ended. Both sides agreed to **resume** _____ .

    A. fighting   B. talking

3. The director is **reviving** a play that has_____

_____.

    A. always been popular with   B. not been performed for forty
          theater audiences   years

4. Evelyn lost the championship to Nina in their last match, and in today's contest _____ will try to **recover** it.

    A. Nina   B. Evelyn

5. You would not expect to _____ paint in an apartment that has just been **renovated**.

    A. smell fresh   B. see peeling

F Consider all the facts below. Then answer the questions.

FACTS

Sam got his wallet back in the Lost and Found. Luckily nothing had been taken.

Sonia was reading a magazine when Allan telephoned. Then she went back to her magazine.

Parker has just put in new shelves and counters. He has modernized the lighting. The store looks altogether different.

Gerald fainted. Charlotte immediately telephoned for an ambulance, but in the excitement she could not remember her own address, so Amy told her.

QUESTIONS

1. Who **renovated** something? 1 _____

2. Who **recovered** something? 2 _____

3. Who needed to be **revived?** 3 _____

4. Who **resumed** something? 4 _____

5. Who could not **recall** something? 5 _____

G *Using Fewer Words.* Replace each italicized expression below with a word that you studied in this lesson.

1. We all hope that you will soon *be well again.* 1 _____

2. The curtain has fallen on Act I, and the play will soon *begin again.* 2 _____

3. With each new success, the hopes that we once had began to *come back to life.* 3 _____

4. Vast sums are spent annually to *restore* our roads and bridges *to good condition.* 4 _____

5. Try to *call back to mind* the exact directions that we were given. 5 _____

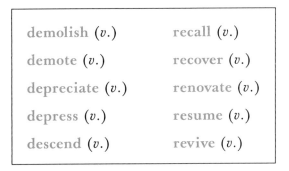

LESSON 27 (Review)

demolish (v.)   recall (v.)

demote (v.)   recover (v.)

depreciate (v.)   renovate (v.)

depress (v.)   resume (v.)

descend (v.)   revive (v.)

A A verb is missing in each passage below. Find that verb in the above box, and write it in the blank space.

1. The plane had begun to _____ for a landing.

2. If you are ill, stay at home until you _____ .

3. That heavy truck could easily _____ a passenger car in a collision.

4. I seem to be suffering from a loss of memory. I cannot _____ anything.

5. They worked hard to _____ the unconscious firefighter.

6. Mrs. Cassidy warned the unruly student that she would _____ him to a lower grade if he did not behave.

7. There has been a power failure, but the lighting company expects service to _____ soon.

8. Cheer up. Do not allow a little mistake to _____ you.

9. Everything here still looks so new that there is no need to _____ the place.

10. My older brother is so jealous of me that if I do anything well, he is sure to _____ it.

B Make sentence (*b*) similar in meaning to sentence (*a*) by inserting *one* word in sentence (*b*). Take that word only from the following box. You may add **s, ed,** or **ing,** if necessary.

appreciate	depress	renovate
ascend	promote	resume
construct	recall	revive
depreciate	regain	

The first answer has been inserted as a sample.

1. (*a*) He was destructive. When I built something, he demolished it.

   (*b*) He was destructive. When I ___constructed___ something, he demolished it.

2. (*a*) After a short rest, she began working again.

   (*b*) After a short rest, she _____ working.

3. (*a*) As the balloon goes up, it looks smaller and smaller.

   (*b*) As the balloon _____ , it looks smaller and smaller.

4. (*a*) This company makes kitchens and bathrooms new again.

   (*b*) This company _____ kitchens and bathrooms.

5. (*a*) Do you expect to be moved to a higher grade?

   (*b*) Do you expect to be _____ ?

6. (*a*) Your accident brings to mind an accident I once had.

   (*b*) Your accident _____ an accident I once had.

7. (*a*) Judy is outstanding. If you call her average, you are belittling her.

   (*b*) Judy is outstanding. If you call her average, you are _____ her.

8. (*a*) The victim could not be brought back to consciousness.

   (*b*) The victim could not be _____ .

9. (a) The house has gone up in value, and the land has gone up, too.

   (b) The house has gone up in value, and the land has _____ , too.

10. (a) Andy is recovering, but the slow healing is discouraging him.

    (b) Andy is recovering, but the slow healing is _____ him.

11. (a) It is hard to get back the trust of someone to whom you have lied.

    (b) It is hard to _____ the trust of someone to whom you have lied.

C You already know how to add suffixes, such as **s, ing, ed,** and **ly.** Now let us learn how to add prefixes.

ADDING PREFIXES: Do not add or drop a letter when you attach a prefix to a word. Keep all the letters of the prefix and all the letters of the word.

PREFIX		WORD		NEW WORD
re	+	elect	=	**reelect** ("elect again")
un	+	able	=	**unable** ("not able")
un	+	natural	=	**unnatural** ("not natural")

Complete the following. The first answer has been entered as a sample.

1. re + admit = __**readmit**__ (*admit again*)

2. re + arrest = _____ (*arrest again*)

3. re + consider = _____ (*consider again*)

4. un + familiar = _____ (*not familiar*)

5. un + aware = _____ (*not aware*)

6. un + important = _____ (*not important*)

7. un + necessary = _____ (*not necessary*)

8. de + frost = _____ (*remove frost from*)

9. de + rail = _____ (*go off the rails*)

10. re + enter = _____ (*enter again*)

D *Adding Prefixes and Suffixes.* Complete the following. The first answer has been entered as a sample.

1. re + capture + ed = <u>**recaptured**</u>
   (*captured again*)

2. re + examine + ed = _____
   (*examined again*)

3. un + open + ed = _____
   (*not opened*)

4. re + open + ed = _____
   (*opened again*)

5. un + use + able = _____
   (*not able to be used*)

6. re + use + able = _____
   (*able to be used again*)

7. de + face + ing = _____
   (*spoiling the looks of*)

8. re + introduce + ing = _____
   (*introducing again*)

9. un + occupy + ed = _____
   (*not occupied*)

10. un + employ + ed = _____
    (*not employed*)

11. re + apply + ing = _____
    (*applying again*)

12. re + apply + s = _____
    (*applies again*)

13. de + grade + ing = _____
    (*lowering the standing of*)

14. un + natural + ly = _____
    (*not naturally*)

15. un + avoid + able = _____
    (*not able to be avoided*)

16. un + avoid + able + ly = _____
    (*in an unavoidable way*)

17. un + hesitate + ing + ly = _____
    (*without hesitating*)

18. re + unite + ed = _____
    (*united again*)

19. de + odor + ize + s = _____
(removes odors)

20. un + expect + ed + ly = _____
(in an unexpected way)

E One word in each sentence below is incomplete. Only a prefix and a suffix are given. You have to fill in the rest of the word, and you will be able to do so if you read carefully. The first word has been completed as a sample.

1. The votes are being re___**count**___ed (counted again).

2. Once a month, Terry **de**_____s (removes the frost from) the refrigerator.

3. Are they **re**_____**ing** (paying back) the money they owe us?

4. The snake has not **re**_____**ed** (appeared again).

5. Yesterday a train **de**_____**ed** (went off the rails).

6. When is the show **re**_____**ing** (opening again)?

7. The watering can has been **re**_____**ed** (filled again).

8. Sometimes, disease **de**_____**s** (spoils the *form*, or shape, of) an arm or leg.

9. You are **de**_____**ing** (spoiling the *face*, or surface, of) the wall with your scribbling.

10. The message has been **de**_____**ed** (changed from *code* to ordinary language).

F Consider each question carefully. Then do the following:

1. Next to **Answer,** write "Yes" or "No."

2. Next to **Explanation,** write one or more good reasons for your "Yes" or "No."

1. A member who dropped out of your club six months ago has heard that the club is going on a trip to Washington, D.C., and wants to rejoin. Would you vote to readmit this member?

   Answer: _____

   Explanation: _____

   _____

   _____

   _____

   _____

   _____

2. With two minutes left to play and the score tied, the star of your team faints, but revives quickly, without help. The star asks to be allowed to stay in the game. The coach is undecided. Should the star be permitted to resume playing?

   Answer: _____

   Explanation: _____

   _____

   _____

   _____

   _____

   _____

3. A classmate who occasionally depreciates your work has just written an excellent story. Would you compliment this classmate?

   Answer: _____

   Explanation: _____

   _____

   _____

   _____

   _____

   _____

G *Listening.* Your teacher will now read an interesting passage to you and give you some questions to answer. Follow your teacher's instructions.

A Pronounce each new word and write it in the space provided. Note:

The *our* in **discourteous** is pronounced ʉr, as in *fur*.

disapproval	dis′ ə proͦov′ ′l	_____
discourteous	dis kʉr′ tē əs	_____
discredit	dis kred′ it	_____
dishearten	dis här′ t′n	_____
disservice	dis sʉr′ vis	_____

B Read carefully and answer the questions.

"I VOTE NO!"

1. I showed my dislike of your motion by voting against it.
   I showed my **disapproval** of your motion by voting against it.

   Disapproval means_____.

2. My brother is polite when we have guests. At other times, he is generally **discourteous**.

   Which word is the opposite of **discourteous**?_____.

   What does **discourteous** mean?_____.

3. His enemies tried to disgrace him.
   His enemies tried to **discredit** him.

   Discredit means_____.

4. By hitting a home run, Naomi encouraged her teammates and **disheartened** the opposition.

   Which word is the opposite of **disheartened**?_____.

   What does **disheartened** mean?_____.

5. Our neighbors did us an ill turn by moving because the new neighbors are very noisy.

   Our neighbors did us a **disservice** by moving because the new neighbors are very noisy.

   Disservice means_____.

DIS: The prefix **dis** means "opposite of" or "not."

dis	+ **hearten**	= **dishearten**
("opposite of")	(meaning "encourage")	("do the opposite of *hearten*"; "discourage")
dis	+ **courteous**	= **discourteous**
("not")		("not courteous")

C Study Your New Words

NEW WORD	WHAT IT MEANS	HOW IT IS USED
disapproval (*n.*) dis′ ə prōōv′ ′l	refusal to approve; unfavorable opinion; dislike *ant.* **approval**	Most of the audience showed their **disapproval** of the film by leaving before it was over. One look of **disapproval** from the parent was enough to stop the child from eating with his fingers.
discourteous (*adj.*) dis kur′ tē əs	not courteous; impolite; rude *ant.* **courteous**	You were **discourteous** to the speaker because you kept reading your newspaper during her talk. It was **discourteous** of you to accept the gift without saying "Thank you."

discredit (v.)	destroy belief or trust in;	Someone tried to
dis kred' it	destroy the reputation of;	**discredit** Paula by
	disgrace	starting a rumor that she
		cheated during the test.
	refuse to accept as true;	Most of us **discredited**
	disbelieve	the rumor, but a few
		believed it.

dishearten (v.)	cause to lose hope;	Your early lead
dis här' t'n	discourage; depress	**disheartened** me and
	ant. **hearten;**	made me feel like giving
	encourage	up.
		Try to be cheerful when
		you speak to the patient.
		Do not say anything that
		might **dishearten** him.

disservice (n.)	injury; harmful or	Dad walks to the station
dis sur' vis	unkind act; ill turn	because he needs the
		exercise. Anyone who
		gives him a ride to the
		train is doing him a
		disservice.
		It is a **disservice** to cut
		down trees that are
		beautiful all year round
		and give us shade in the
		summer.

D Which choice, *A* or *B*, makes the sentence correct? Write the correct word or words in the blank space.

1. Your telephone call last night was a **disservice** because it _____

_____ .

    A. helped me get a higher   B. awoke me, and I could not fall
        score on today's test   asleep again

2. The fans expressed their **disapproval** by _____ .

    A. booing   B. applauding

3. It would **dishearten** me if I were _____ .

    A. promoted   B. demoted

4. I met a **discourteous** person who answered "_____

_____" when I said "How are you?"

    A. It's none of your business!   B. Fine, thank you. How have you been?

5. You **discredited** me when you told Joe that I was _____.

    A. generally obliging   B. seldom generous

E   Form twenty new **dis** words by completing the following. The first answer has been entered as a sample.

1. dis	+	honest	=	**dishonest**	(*not honest*)
2. dis	+	agree	=	_____	(*fail to agree*)
3. dis	+	similar	=	_____	(*not similar; unlike*)
4. dis	+	place	=	_____	(*take the place of; replace*)
5. dis	+	respect	=	_____	(*lack of respect; rudeness*)
6. dis	+	please	=	_____	(*make angry; annoy*)
7. dis	+	continue	=	_____	(*put an end to*)
8. dis	+	close	=	_____	(*make known; reveal*)
9. dis	+	infect	=	_____	(*remove disease germs from*)
10. dis	+	satisfy	=	_____	(*fail to satisfy*)
11. dis	+	regard	=	_____	(*pay no regard or attention to; ignore*)
12. dis	+	connect	=	_____	(*undo the connection of; separate*)
13. dis	+	arm	=	_____	(*take away weapons from*)
14. dis	+	obey	=	_____	(*fail to obey*)
15. dis	+	loyal	=	_____	(*not loyal; not faithful*)
16. dis	+	organize	=	_____	(*upset the normal arrangement of; throw into confusion*)

17. dis + appear = _____ (*pass from sight*)

18. dis + approve = _____ (*refuse to approve; reject*)

19. dis + able = _____ (*make unable to move, act, or work normally; weaken*)

20. dis + qualify = _____ (*make unable to do something; declare unfit*)

F One word in each sentence below is incomplete. Only a prefix and a suffix are given. Fill in the rest of the word. The first word has been completed as a sample.

1. The results dis __satisfi__ ed (*failed to satisfy*) us.

2. Why are you **dis**_____ing (*failing to obey*) the rules?

3. A severe storm usually **dis**_____s (*upsets the normal arrangement of*) our lives.

4. Who accused you of **dis**_____ty (*not being honest*)?

5. One of the dog's legs was **dis**_____ed (*weakened*) by an accident.

6. Someone has been **dis**_____ing (*undoing the connection between*) the wires.

7. We **dis**_____ed (*failed to agree*).

8. You were **dis**_____ful (*lacking in respect*) to our guest of honor.

9. My mother **dis**_____s (*refuses to approve*) of my not eating a full breakfast.

10. Benedict Arnold is remembered for his **dis**_____ty (*not being loyal*).

11. Supermarkets are **dis**_____ing (*taking the place of*) small shops.

12. Their unfair charges **dis**_____ed (*annoyed*) us.

13. Who has been **dis**_____ing (*making known*) our secrets?

14. He generally **dis**_____s (*pays no attention to*) instructions.

15. The twins look alike but they behave **dis**_____**ly** (*in unlike ways*).

16. She **dis**_____**s** (*removes disease germs from*) her plants with a garden spray.

17. The police **dis**_____**ed** (*took the weapons away from*) the thugs.

18. See how the sun is **dis**_____**ing** (*dropping from sight*) in the west.

19. Your sprained ankle **dis**_____**s** (*makes unfit*) you from playing in today's game.

20. They are **dis**_____**ing** (*putting an end to*) their quarrel.

G Read all the statements in the boxes below. Then answer the questions.

> Erica was discouraged to learn that she had been dropped from the team because of her failure in two subjects. Maria has taken her place.

> Carl put out a loosely tied bundle of newspapers that the wind scattered all over the neighborhood.

> During my talk, George kept whispering to his friend Martin until Mrs. Alderman gave him a stern look.

> Fred gave Rose some gossip to the effect that the Di Nardos might be selling their home, but she told him she didn't believe it.

1. Who performed a **disservice?**   1 _____

2. Who was **disqualified?**   2 _____

3. Who **discredited** something?   3 _____

4. Who was **discourteous?**   4 _____

5. Who expressed **disapproval?**   5 _____

6. Who was **disheartened?**   6 _____

7. Who **displaced** someone?   7 _____

A Pronounce each new word and write it in the space provided.

misconception	mis' kən sep' shən	_____
misgiving	mis giv' ing	_____
misinform	mis in fôrm'	_____
misjudge	mis juj'	_____
mismanage	mis man' ij	_____

B Read carefully and answer the questions.

1. You have a wrong idea of how our government works.
   You have a **misconception** of how our government works.

   Misconception means_____.

2. The test pilot had some feeling of doubt about the new plane.
   The test pilot had some **misgiving** about the new plane.

   Misgiving means_____.

3. We try not to give wrong or misleading information to anyone.
   We try not to **misinform** anyone.

   Misinform means_____.

4. You did not catch the ball because you judged it wrongly.
   You did not catch the ball because you **misjudged** it.

   Misjudged means_____.

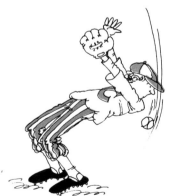

5. A firm that is badly managed may have to go out of business.
   A firm that is **mismanaged** may have to go out of business.

   Mismanaged means_____.

MIS: The prefix **mis** means "wrong," or "wrongly," "bad," or "badly."

mis +	**conception** =	**misconception**
("wrong")	("idea")	("wrong idea")
mis +	**manage** =	**mismanage**
("badly")		("manage badly")

C Study Your New Words

NEW WORD	WHAT IT MEANS	HOW IT IS USED
misconception (*n.*) mis′ kən sep′ shən	mistaken idea; wrong conception; misunderstanding	Before the voyages of Columbus, people had the **misconception** that the earth was flat. Some people think it is very easy to take care of a dog. I wonder how they got this **misconception.**
misgiving (*n.*) mis giv′ ing	feeling of doubt, fear, or suspicion	I took the part with some **misgivings** because I had never acted on a stage before an audience. We can postpone our trip until tomorrow if you have any **misgiving** about today's weather.
misinform (*v.*) mis in fôrm′	give wrong or misleading information to	You told me the key was under the doormat, but it was not there. You **misinformed** me. I am not good at giving directions, so please ask someone else. I do not want to **misinform** you.

misjudge (v.) mis juj′	judge wrongly	I **misjudged** the amount of milk remaining in the refrigerator. I thought we had about a half gallon, but there was less than a quart.
	judge unjustly	We cannot understand your dislike for Joe. He is really a fine fellow. You must have **misjudged** him.
mismanage (v.) mis man′ ij	manage badly or improperly	Wendy could not finish her homework because she had watched TV too long. She had **mismanaged** her time.
		Jimmy **mismanages** his allowance. He spends all of it the first day and has nothing left for the rest of the week.

D Which choice, *A* or *B*, makes the sentence correct? Write the correct word or words in the blank space.

1. If it costs you fifteen cents to make a glass of lemonade and you sell it for

_____ cents, you are **mismanaging** your business.

   A. fifteen   B. twenty

2. I **misjudged** Dora. I thought she was familiar with the game, but she turned out

   to be _____ .

   A. a novice   B. an expert

3. _____ are full of **misgivings**.

   A. Optimists   B. Pessimists

4. You **misinformed** us when you said the library closes at six. We got there at 6:15

   and it was _____ .

   A. closed   B. open

5. It is a **misconception** to believe that everyone _____

_____.

   A. needs food in order to live   B. is honest and kind

E Form twenty new **mis** words by completing the following. The first answer has been entered as a sample.

1. mis + place = __misplace_____ (*put in a wrong place*)

2. mis + deed = _____ (*wrong or wicked act*)

3. mis + pronounce = _____ (*pronounce incorrectly*)

4. mis + spell = _____ (*spell incorrectly*)

5. mis + direct = _____ (*give wrong directions to*)

6. mis + interpret = _____ (*understand or explain wrongly*)

7. mis + carry = _____ (*be unsuccessful; go wrong*)

8. mis + behave = _____ (*behave badly*)

9. mis + handle = _____ (*handle badly or roughly*)

10. mis + fortune = _____ (*unlucky accident*)

11. mis + guide = _____ (*lead astray*)

12. mis + print = _____ (*make a mistake in printing*)

13. mis + treat = _____ (*treat badly*)

14. mis + calculate = _____ (*make a mistake in arithmetic or planning*)

15. mis + rule = _____ (*rule badly or unwisely*)

16. mis + trust = _____ (*have no faith or confidence in*)

17. mis + fire = _____ (*fail to fire or explode properly*)

18. mis + use = _____ (*use for the wrong purpose*)

19. mis + quote = _____ (*repeat the words of another person wrongly*)

20. mis + match = _____ (*match badly*)

F One word in each sentence below is incomplete. Only a prefix and a suffix are given. Fill in the rest of the word. The first word has been completed as a sample.

1. No one was mis__treat____ed (*treated badly*).

2. She always **mis**_____s (*wrongly spells*) my name.

3. He **mis**_____ed (*had no confidence in*) us.

4. I think we are being **mis**_____ed (*given wrong directions*).

5. My application was **mis**_____ed (*put in the wrong place*).

6. The children are not **mis**_____ing (*behaving badly*).

7. I must have **mis**_____ed (*made a mistake in arithmetic*).

8. This toy must not be **mis**_____ed (*roughly handled*) because it can break easily.

9. You have **mis**_____ed (*wrongly explained*) what has happened.

10. They are **mis**_____ing (*leading astray*) us.

11. She **mis**_____ed (*did not correctly repeat the words of*) my statement.

12. Joel always **mis**_____s (*wrongly pronounces*) your name.

13. This is a **mis**_____ed (*badly matched*) pair because one of the socks is a different color from the other.

14. The newspaper **mis**_____ed (*made a mistake in printing*) her name.

15. A leader who **mis**_____s (*unwisely rules*) a nation should not be reelected.

16. **Mis**_____s (*wicked acts*) should not go unpunished.

17. The treasurer is **mis**_____ing (*using for the wrong purpose*) our club's money.

18. The bear escaped when Penny's rifle **mis**_____ed (*failed to fire properly*).

19. We had a number of **mis**_____s (*unlucky accidents*).

20. All of our plans **mis**_____ed (*went wrong*).

G Read the statements in all the boxes. Then answer the questions below them.

Blanche deliberately told Reggie she is about a mile from his house. The fact is she is more than two miles away.

Nick's vegetable plants died because he did not give them enough water.

Rose warned Allan that it was going to rain heavily, but he did not worry.

Olga thought that Rachel was not good enough for our team, so the other side picked her and, surprisingly, she won the game for them.

It is hard to understand where Barbara got the idea that all the tickets had been sold because the box office still had plenty of them.

---

1. Who was **misjudged**? 1 _____

2. Who **misinformed** someone? 2 _____

3. Who had no **misgivings**? 3 _____

4. Who had a **misconception** about another person? 4 _____

5. Who **mismanaged** something? 5 _____

6. Who has a **misconception** about something? 6 _____

LESSON 30 (Review)

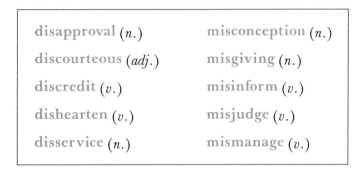

disapproval (*n.*)	misconception (*n.*)
discourteous (*adj.*)	misgiving (*n.*)
discredit (*v.*)	misinform (*v.*)
dishearten (*v.*)	misjudge (*v.*)
disservice (*n.*)	mismanage (*v.*)

A   A word is missing in each passage below. Find that word in the above box, and write it in the blank space.

1. Some germs are so useful that we would not be able to live without them. So it is a _____ to think that all germs are harmful.

2. Our new car was so badly damaged that it would _____ you to see it.

3. You are sure to _____ a book if you judge it only by its cover.

4. When we went up to ask a question, the person in charge said, "Get away from here!" Did you ever hear anything so _____ ?

5. You did me a _____ when you stopped me to introduce me to your friends. As a result of the delay, I missed my bus.

6. My rival wants to damage my reputation, so she is looking for ways to _____ _____ me.

7. We do not worry much about the present, but we have some _____ about the future.

8. Many riders showed their _____ of the fare increase by bicycling to work.

9. He knows nothing about running a picnic. If we put him in charge, he will probably _____ it.

10. You told us admission to the play was free, but we had to pay to get in. Why did you _____ us?

B *Using Fewer Words*. Which word from the box at the beginning of this lesson can take the place of the italicized words? Write that word in the space provided, adding *s, ing, ed,* or *ly,* if necessary.

1. We have *feelings of doubt* about the outcome.

1 _____

2. You have done us another *ill turn*.

2 _____

3. My rival is *not managing* her campaign *properly*.

3 _____

4. They treated us *in a rude way*.

4 _____

5. You have *judged* us *unjustly*.

5 _____

6. Where did you get the *mistaken idea* that I am to blame?

6 _____

7. His *unfavorable opinion* of our plan is no surprise.

7 _____

8. It always *makes* me *feel depressed* to hear you complain.

8 _____

9. She has been *giving* us *wrong information*.

9 _____

10. The rumor was *not believed*.

10 _____

C Each unfinished word below has both a prefix and a suffix missing. Enter the missing prefix and suffix. Choose all your prefixes and suffixes from the following box:

de	dis	mis	re	un
ed	ing	ly	s	

The first unfinished word has been completed as a sample.

1. She seldom ——**mis**—pronounce——**s**—— (*incorrectly pronounces*) a word.

2. Tom generally _____**regard**_____ (*pays no attention to*) what we say.

3. The weather forecasts have been _____**inform**_____ (*giving wrong information to*) us.

4. Have you _____**frost**_____ (*removed the frost from*) your refrigerator?

5. The envelope was _____**open**_____ (*not opened*).

6. The waiter is _____**fill**_____ (*filling again*) your glass.

7. They have been dealing with us _____**honest**_____ (*in a way that is not honest*).

8. Paul _____**agree**_____ (*did not agree*) with us.

9. Stewart _____**face**_____ (*spoiled the surface of*) the desk by scratching his initials on it.

10. I doubt that any of our members ever behaved _____**loyal**_____ (*in a way that is not loyal*).

11. I hope she _____**cover**_____ (*gets her health back*) soon.

12. The last word in your sentence is _____**spell**_____ (*not spelled correctly*).

13. Why are you _____**count**_____ (*counting again*) your money?

14. One book was _____**place**_____ (*put in the wrong place*).

15. He did not play because he was _____**qualify**_____ (*declared unfit*).

16. We _____**calculate**_____ (*made a mistake in planning*).

17. The patient looked _____**natural**_____ (*in a way that was not natural*) pale.

18. Is the fog _____**appear**_____ (*passing from sight*)?

19. Everything _____**please**_____ (*fails to please*) them.

20. I think you _____**quote**_____ (*incorrectly repeated*) my words.

D *Synonyms and Antonyms:* For each italicized word or expression on line (*a*), enter a *synonym* on line (*b*), and an *antonym* on line (*c*).

Choose all your synonyms and antonyms from the following list. You may add **s, ing, ed,** or **ly,** if necessary.

appreciate	demolish	disclose	forget
approval	demote	discourteous	polite
ascend	depreciate	dislike	promote
conceal	depress	dissimilar	recall
construct	descend	encourage	same

The answers to the first question have been entered as a sample.

1. (*a*) Some are being *moved down in rank*.
   (*b*) Some are being __**demoted**__.
   (*c*) Others are being __**promoted**__.

2. (a) Everything has been *revealed*.

   (b) Everything has been _____ .

   (c) Nothing is being _____ .

3. (a) A few behaved *rudely*.

   (b) A few behaved _____ .

   (c) But most people acted _____ .

4. (a) I cannot *remember* details.

   (b) I cannot _____ details.

   (c) I _____ details easily.

5. (a) My plan met with their *disapproval*.

   (b) My plan met with their _____ .

   (c) Her plan won their _____ .

6. (a) We are *building* a new stadium.

   (b) We are _____ a new stadium.

   (c) We are _____ the old stadium.

7. (a) Pat and I used *different* methods.

   (b) Pat and I used _____ methods.

   (c) But we both got the _____ answer.

8. (a) Bad news *disheartens* us.

   (b) Bad news _____ us.

   (c) Good news _____ us.

9. (a) The elevator *went up* to the top floor.

   (b) The elevator _____ to the top floor.

   (c) The elevator _____ to the basement.

10. (a) Some things have *gone down in value*.

    (b) Some things have _____ .

    (c) But land has _____ .

E *Listening.* Your teacher will now read an interesting passage to you and give you some questions to answer. Follow your teacher's instructions.

Dictionary of the Words Taught in This Book

abundant (*adj.*)
ə bun′ dənt

plentiful; more than enough; not scarce

Water is scarce. Our reservoirs are nearly empty. We will be in trouble unless we get an **abundant** amount of rain soon.

acknowledge (*v.*)
ək näl′ ij

admit the truth or existence of; admit; confess
   ant. **deny**

I will gladly **acknowledge** my mistake if you can show me that I am wrong.

make known that something has been received or noticed

She **acknowledged** my gift by sending me a thank-you card.

adolescent (*n.*)
ad′ ə les′ ′nt

person between childhood and adulthood; teenager

Lori, who is 13, is not the only **adolescent** in the family. Her sister Lynne is 16, and her brother Roger is 19.

adore (*v.*)
ə dôr′

like very much; be extremely fond of; worship

The performers are not popular with everyone. Their fans **adore** them, but there are people who detest them.

alert (*adj.*)
ə lʉrt′

watchful and ready to act quickly; wide-awake

The **alert** cook saw that the pot was going to boil over and quickly removed it from the stove.

alter (*v.*)
ôl′ tər

make partly but not completely different; change in some way

If my sister buys a dress that is too long, my mother **alters** it by taking up the hem.

become different; change

Oliver is taller and heavier than he was two years ago; but otherwise he has not **altered**.

149

altogether (*adv.*) ôl′ tə ge*th*′ ər	completely; wholly	Her excuse for coming late was **altogether** incredible.
	on the whole; considering everything	We won five games and lost two. **Altogether,** it was a good season.
annually (*adv.*) an′ yoo wəl ē	each year; yearly	To rent a garage, some people pay $50 a month, or $600 **annually**.
apparently (*adv.*) ə per′ ənt lē	obviously; evidently; as far as one can see	It was past midnight. All the lights in the house were out. Everyone was **apparently** asleep.
appreciate (*v.*) ə prē′ shē āt	become more valuable; go up in price	A car bought fifty years ago for a few hundred dollars is worth thousands now because it is an antique. It has **appreciated** in value.
approval (*n.*) ə prōō′ v′l	favorable opinion	The audience showed its **approval** of our performance by applauding.
arduous (*adj.*) är′ joo wəs	hard to do; difficult *ant.* **easy**	Adding long columns of numbers without a calculator is an **arduous** task.
	using up a great deal of energy; strenuous	If running is too **arduous** for you, try jogging.
artificial (*adj.*) är′ tə fish′ əl	not natural; made by human beings rather than nature *ant.* **natural**	I would never have thought the flowers were **artificial** because they looked so natural.
	false; pretended; not sincere	When people greet you with an **artificial** smile, you can tell they are not overjoyed to see you.

ascend (*v.*) ə send′	climb; go up	We **ascended** Mt. Washington on Thursday and descended the next morning.
awkward (*adj.*) ôk′ wərd	not skillful; not graceful; clumsy *ant.* **skillful; graceful**	With coaching, an **awkward** batter can become a skillful hitter.
	difficult; uncomfortable; embarrassing	My neighbors saw me as I was searching for my ball in their flower garden. It was an **awkward** situation.
belittle (*v.*) bi lit′ ′l	make seem little or unimportant; depreciate	Romeo's friend received a bad wound but he **belittled** it. He called it a scratch.
benefit (*v.*) ben′ ə fit	do good to or for; help; aid *ant.* **harm**	Rest **benefits** a person who has a cold.
	receive good; be helped; profit	If you have learned something from your past mistakes, you have **benefited** from them.
blunder (*n.*) blun′ dər	careless or foolish mistake; error	The salesclerk made a **blunder** and gave me a dollar too much, but I gave it back to her.
boring (*adj.*) bôr′ ing	tiresome and uninteresting; dull *ant.* **interesting**	My vacation was so **boring** that I was glad when it was over.
clash (*v.*) klash	disagree sharply; be not in harmony	The workers and their employer **clashed** over wages. A strike followed.
clumsy (*adj.*) klum′ zē	awkward in movement; not graceful; not skillful	The **clumsy** dancer stepped on his partner's foot.

compensate (*v.*) käm′ pən sāt	pay	Some firms pay their employees weekly, and some **compensate** them monthly.
	make amends (make up for injury or loss that one has caused)	Harvey wants to **compensate** for losing his temper. He is willing to apologize.
competitor (*n.*) kəm pet′ ə tər	person who takes part in a contest; rival	So far Charlene is the only one running for vice-president. She has no **competitor.**
compliment (*v.*) käm′ plə mənt	offer a word of praise or admiration to; congratulate	We **complimented** the hostess for her delicious cake.
conceal (*v.*) kən sēl′	put out of sight; keep secret; hide	Ben Gunn learned where the pirates had **concealed** their treasure.
	ant. **reveal**	When we have good news, we are eager to **reveal** it. When it is bad, we may **conceal** it for a while.
conception (*n.*) kən sep′ shən	idea	Before the voyages of Columbus, most people had the **conception** that the earth was flat.
conserve (*v.*) kən sɤrv′	keep from being used up or wasted; save *ant.* **waste**	One way to **conserve** electricity is to turn off the lights in rooms that are not in use.
considerably (*adv.*) kən sid′ ər ə blē	a great deal; much	Prices went up **considerably.**
construct (*v.*) kən strukt′	build; put together	It does not make sense to demolish a building that was **constructed** only a short time ago.

courteous (*adj.*)
kur′ tē əs

polite; thoughtful of others

It was **courteous** of you to hold the door for the people who were behind us.

culprit (*n.*)
kul′ prit

person who has committed a fault or crime; offender

Two people were killed in the crash, but the **culprit,** a drunken driver, was not seriously hurt.

currently (*adv.*)
kur′ ənt lē

at the present time; now

The pen you bought last week for $2.95 is **currently** selling for $1.95.

deceive (*v.*)
di sēv′

make (someone) believe what is not true; deal dishonestly with; mislead

Amanda thought that her daughter was attending school, but that was not true. The girl had been **deceiving** her.

ant. **enlighten**

Let me **enlighten** you about these diamonds. They are artificial. I do not want you to be **deceived.**

decode (*v.*)
dē kōd′

translate from *code* (secret writing) to ordinary language

The secret message has been **decoded.** Now we know its meaning.

deface (*v.*)
di fās′

spoil the appearance of

You are **defacing** the wall with your scribbling.

deform (*v.*)
di fôrm′

spoil the form or shape of

Sometimes disease **deforms** an arm or leg.

defrost (*v.*)
di frôst′

remove the frost from

Once a month, Terry **defrosts** the refrigerator.

degrade (*v.*)
di grād′

lower the standing of; disgrace

Rose felt she would **degrade** herself if she cheated in the test.

demolish (*v.*)
di mäl′ ish

tear down; raze; smash; destroy
ant. **construct;**
build

Several homes built only a few years ago are being **demolished** to make way for the new expressway.

demote (*v.*) di mōt′	reduce or move down to a lower grade or rank *ant.* **promote**	If you do well, you will be **promoted,** and if you do not, you may be **demoted,** or even dismissed.
deny (*v.*) di nī′	say something is not true; refuse to acknowledge	The suspect acknowledges that he was present at the scene of the crime, but he **denies** that he did anything wrong.
deodorize (*v.*) dē ō′ dər īz	remove odors from	A good way to **deodorize** a room is to open some windows.
dependent (*n.*) di pen′ dənt	person who is supported by someone else	If you do not support yourself, you are a **dependent**.
depreciate (*v.*) di prē′ shē āt	go down in value or price *ant.* **appreciate**	The new car that Dad bought recently has **depreciated**. It is worth less now. But a 50-year- old car that sold for a few hundred dollars when it was new is now worth thousands because it is an antique. It has **appreciated**.
	make seem unimportant; belittle	She has a good record, but she calls herself a failure. She is always **depreciating** herself.
depress (*v.*) di pres′	press down	When you are learning to play the guitar, it may hurt your fingers at first as you **depress** the strings.
	make gloomy or sad; discourage; sadden	We lost 7-0. The defeat **depressed** us.
derail (*v.*) di rāl′	go, or cause to go, off the rails	Yesterday, a train **derailed**.

descend (*v.*)
di send′

move down from a higher to a lower place; go down; climb down

    ant. **ascend; climb**

Hold on to the banister as you **descend** the staircase.

We **ascended** the mountain on Thursday morning and **descended** the following afternoon.

detest (*v.*)
di test′

dislike very much; hate
    ant. **adore**

If you deceive people, they will grow to **detest** you.

disable (*v.*)
dis ā′ b'l

make unable to move; weaken

One of the dog's legs was **disabled** by an accident.

disappear (*v.*)
dis ə pir′

drop from sight; vanish

See how the sun is **disappearing** in the west.

disapproval (*n.*)
dis′ ə prōōv′ 'l

refusal to approve; unfavorable opinion; dislike
    ant. **approval**

Most of the audience showed their **disapproval** of the film by leaving before it was over.

disapprove (*v.*)
dis ə prōōv′

refuse to approve; have an opinion against

My mother **disapproves** of my not eating a full breakfast.

disarm (*v.*)
dis ärm′

take away weapons from

The police **disarmed** the thugs.

disbelieve (*v.*)
dis bə lēv′

refuse to believe

We have reason to **disbelieve** the claim because it was made by someone we do not trust.

disclose (*v.*)
dis klōz′

make known; reveal

Who has been **disclosing** our secrets?

disconnect (*v.*)
dis kə nekt′

undo the connection between

Someone has been **disconnecting** the wires.

discontinue (*v.*)
dis′ kən tin′ yōō

put an end to

They are **discontinuing** their quarrel.

discourteous (*adj.*)
dis kur′ tē əs

not courteous; impolite; rude
    ant. **courteous**

It was **discourteous** of you to accept the gift without saying "Thank you."

Dictionary 155

discredit (*v.*) dis kred′ it	destroy belief or trust in; destroy the reputation of; disgrace	Someone tried to **discredit** Paula by starting a rumor that she cheated during the test.
	refuse to accept as true; disbelieve	Most of us **discredited** the rumor, but a few believed it.
dishearten (*v.*) dis här′ t'n	cause to lose hope; discourage; depress *ant.* **hearten; encourage**	Try to be cheerful when you speak to the patient. Do not say anything that might **dishearten** him.
disinfect (*v.*) dis′ in fekt′	remove disease germs from	She **disinfects** her plants with a garden spray.
disloyal (*adj.*) dis loi′ əl	not loyal; not faithful; faithless	Benedict Arnold is remembered for being **disloyal** to his country.
disobey (*v.*) dis ə bā′	fail to obey; refuse to obey	Why are you **disobeying** the rules?
disorganize (*v.*) dis ôr′ gə nīz	upset the normal arrangement of	A severe storm usually **disorganizes** our lives.
displace (*v.*) dis plās′	take the place of	Supermarkets are **displacing** small shops.
display (*v.*) dis plā′	put or spread out to attract attention; put on view; exhibit	The T-shirt I wanted was **displayed** in the store window.
	show; reveal *ant.* **conceal**	Dad **displayed** his annoyance with my sister when he told her not to smoke in the house.
displease (*v.*) dis plēz′	not please; annoy; make angry	Their unfair charges **displeased** us.
disposition (*n.*) dis′ pə zish′ ən	person's general attitude toward things; mood; outlook	A customer who has to wait nearly an hour on a checkout line is not likely to be in a good **disposition**.

disqualify (*v.*) dis kwäl′ ə fī	make unfit	Your sprained ankle **disqualifies** you from playing in today's game.
disregard (*v.*) dis′ ri gärd′	pay no attention or regard to; ignore	He generally **disregards** instructions.
disrespectful (*adj.*) dis′ ri spekt′ f′l	lacking in respect; impolite	You were **disrespectful** to our guest of honor.
dissatisfy (*v.*) dis sat′ is fī	fail to satisfy	The results **dissatisfied** us.
disservice (*n.*) dis sʉr′ vis	injury; harmful or unkind act; ill turn	It is a **disservice** to cut down trees that are beautiful all year round and give us shade in the summer.
dissimilar (*adj.*) di sim′ ə lər	not alike; different	The twins look alike but they behave in **dissimilar** ways.
embarrassing (*adj.*) im bar′ ə sing	causing uneasiness or shame; awkward	A classmate greeted me by my first name, but I could not remember hers. It was an **embarrassing** situation for me.
encounter (*v.*) in koun′ tər	come face to face with; come upon; meet	There are supposed to be deer in these woods, but so far we have not **encountered** any.
enlighten (*v.*) in līt′ ′n	furnish with knowledge or truth; inform	Let me **enlighten** you about these diamonds. They are artificial. I do not want you to be deceived.
evidently (*adv.*) ev′ ə dənt lē	obviously; apparently; clearly	The sun was beginning to reappear. **Evidently,** the showers were ending.
familiar (*adj.*) fə mil′ yər	well-known; easily recognized; common *ant.* **strange**	Skyscrapers are a **familiar** sight to those who live in big cities.

	well acquainted; having a good knowledge of	I am not **familiar** with this machine. Please show me how to operate it.
fragment (*n.*) frag′ mənt	part broken off from a whole; small piece	Betty broke her crackers into **fragments** and put them into her soup.
generally (*adv.*) jen′ ər ə lē	usually; in most cases; as a rule	I am surprised that Ginny is not here yet because she **generally** gets home before me.
generous (*adj.*) jen′ ər əs	willing to share with others; unselfish ant. **stingy**	Our **generous** neighbors told us that we are welcome to swim in their backyard pool.
	large; plentiful	For dessert, I was served a **generous** slice of watermelon.
graceful (*adj.*) grās′ fəl	beautiful in movement, form, or manner; not awkward	It is a pleasure to watch birds in flight. They are so **graceful**.
gradually (*adv.*) graj′ oo wə lē	bit by bit; little by little; slowly ant. **suddenly**	We did not know each other at first, but we **gradually** became friends.
gratify (*v.*) grat′ ə fī	please; give pleasure to ant. **disappoint**	We like to be complimented. A word of praise **gratifies** us and makes us try harder.
	give in to; satisfy	Babies are quick to cry if some of their wishes are not immediately **gratified**.
grieve (*v.*) grēv	feel deep grief or sorrow; be sad; mourn ant. **rejoice**	The whole town **grieved** for the victims of the crash.
	cause to feel grief; sadden	Our defeat in the championship game **grieves** us, but the victors are **rejoicing**.

guest (*n.*) gest	person entertained in another person's home; visitor	Gloria will be my **guest** on Saturday. She is coming to my house for lunch.
	person treated to a meal or other entertainment	When someone invites you to a theater or a restaurant, you are not expected to pay because you are a **guest**.
harmonize (*v.*) här′ mə nīz	be in *harmony* (agreement); agree; go together in a pleasant way *ant.* **clash**	Tennis shoes are all right with a sports outfit, but they do not **harmonize** with a bridal gown.
	bring into harmony or agreement	We are so far apart that it seems impossible to **harmonize** our opinions.
harmony (*n.*) här′ mə nē	agreement in ideas, actions, and feelings; peace and friendship	Occasionally there was some disagreement in our committee, but most of the time we worked in **harmony**.
hearsay (*n.*) hir′ sā	something one has heard which may or may not be true; gossip; rumor	There is a report that this building has been sold. I don't know whether it is true or just **hearsay**.
hesitate (*v.*) hez′ ə tāt	wait or stop for a moment; fail to act promptly; pause	The house could have burned to the ground if the owner had **hesitated** in calling the fire department.
hobby (*n.*) häb′ ē	spare-time activity that one likes to do or work at; pastime	Farmers raise vegetables for a living, but we grow them as a **hobby**.
horizon (*n.*) hə rī′ z'n	line where the sky seems to meet the earth or the sea	No one can see beyond the **horizon**.
	limit of a person's knowledge, experience, or outlook	Reading broadens a person's **horizon**.

host (*n.*) hōst	person who entertains guests at home, or pays for their entertainment at a restaurant or theater	A good **host** or **hostess** tries to make the guests feel welcome.
hostess (*n.*) hōs′ tis	Note that **host** is used for a male, and **hostess** for a female.	Mr. and Mrs. Smith have invited us. He is a witty **host,** and she is a very kind **hostess**.
imitate (*v.*) im′ ə tāt	try to be like or act like; copy	Younger children **imitate** their older brothers and sisters.
	act like, in fun; mimic	Dalma got a great deal of applause when she **imitated** some famous comedy stars.
impatient (*adj.*) im pā′ shənt	not willing to put up with delay or bother; easily annoyed	When the line at the checkout counter did not move, some of the customers became **impatient** and left.
	eager for something to happen; restless	Everyone was **impatient** for the game to begin.
incredible (*adj.*) in kred′ ə b'l	unbelievable; hard to believe	Computers can give us answers with **incredible** speed.
intersection (*n.*) in′ tər sek′ shən	place where two or more things—for example, streets—cross; crossing	A very young child needs to be accompanied by an adult when crossing a dangerous **intersection**.
lately (*adv.*) lāt′ lē	not long ago	I am familiar with the movie because I saw it **lately**.
	recently	We used to see Lori almost every day, but we have not encountered her **lately**.
legible (*adj.*) lej′ ə b'l	easy to read; clear enough to be read; readable	Most typed reports are more **legible** than handwritten ones.

| **leisure** (*n.*)
lē′ zhər | free time; time to do the things you like to do | It is a mistake to spend all of your **leisure** watching TV. |

leisure (*n.*)
lē′ zhər

free time; time to do the things you like to do

It is a mistake to spend all of your **leisure** watching TV.

mimic (*v.*)
mim′ ik

copy closely so as to make fun of; imitate

At the party, Rosemary **mimicked** her teacher's way of talking. Everyone, including the teacher, laughed.

misbehave (*v.*)
mis′ bə hāv′

behave badly

The children are not **misbehaving**.

miscalculate (*v.*)
mis kal′ kyə lāt

make a mistake in arithmetic or planning

I got the wrong answer. I must have **miscalculated.**

miscarry (*v.*)
mis kar′ ē

go wrong

All our plans **miscarried**. Nothing turned out right.

misconception (*n.*)
mis′ kən sep′ shən

mistaken idea; wrong conception; misunderstanding

Some people think it is very easy to take care of a dog. I wonder how they got this **misconception.**

misdeed (*n.*)
mis dēd′

wrong or wicked deed; crime

Misdeeds should not go unpunished.

misdirect (*v.*)
mis də rekt′

direct wrongly; give wrong directions to

I think we are being **misdirected.**

misfire (*v.*)
mis fīr′

fail to go off; fail to fire properly

The bear escaped when Penny's rifle **misfired.**

misgiving (*n.*)
mis giv′ ing

feeling of doubt, fear, or suspicion

We can postpone our trip until tomorrow if you have any **misgiving** about today's weather.

mishandle (*v.*)
mis han′ d'l

handle badly or roughly

This toy must not be **mishandled** because it can break easily.

mishap (*n.*)
mis′ hap

unlucky accident

We had a number of **mishaps** that prevented us from completing our work on time.

misinform (*v.*) mis in fôrm′	give wrong or misleading information to	I am not good at giving directions, so please ask someone else. I do not want to **misinform** you.
misinterpret (*v.*) mis′ in tʉr′ prit	explain or understand in a wrong way	You have **misinterpreted** what has happened.
misjudge (*v.*) mis juj′	judge wrongly	I **misjudged** the amount of milk remaining in the refrigerator. I thought we had about a half gallon, but there was less than a quart.
	judge unjustly	We cannot understand your dislike for Joe. He is really a fine fellow. You must have **misjudged** him.
mislead (*v.*) mis lēd′	lead in a wrong direction; lead astray	You are **misleading** us. Let's get back to the right track.
mismanage (*v.*) mis man′ ij	manage badly or improperly	Jimmy **mismanages** his allowance. He spends all of it the first day and has nothing left for the rest of the week.
mismatched (*adj.*) mis macht′	badly matched	This is a **mismatched** pair because one of the socks is a different color from the other.
misplace (*v.*) mis plās′	put in the wrong place	My application was **misplaced.** I hope it will soon be found.
misprint (*v.*) mis print′	print incorrectly	The newspaper **misprinted** her name.
mispronounce (*v.*) mis prə nouns′	pronounce wrongly	Joel always **mispronounces** your name.
misquote (*v.*) mis kwōt′	repeat the words of another person wrongly	She **misquoted** my statement.

misrule (*v.*) mis rool′	rule in a bad or unfair manner; misgovern	A leader who **misrules** a nation should not be reelected.
misspell (*v.*) mis spel′	spell incorrectly	She always **misspells** my name.
mistreat (*v.*) mis trēt′	treat badly	Everyone was dealt with fairly. No one was **mistreated.**
mistrust (*v.*) mis trust′	have no faith or confidence in; distrust	He did not leave his watch and wallet with us. He **mistrusted** us.
misuse (*v.*) mis yōōz′	use for the wrong purpose	The treasurer is **misusing** our club's money.
mood (*n.*) mōōd	state of mind (the way a person feels); disposition	Sally is in a cheerful **mood** because her vacation starts tomorrow.
natural (*adj.*) nach′ ər əl	produced by nature, rather than by human beings; not artificial	Cotton and wool are **natural** materials, but nylon and dacron are artificial.
negligent (*adj.*) neg′ li jənt	failing to use proper care; careless *ant.* **careful**	I dialed the wrong number because I was **negligent.** I should have paid more attention to what I was doing.
novice (*n.*) näv′ is	person who is new at something; beginner *ant.* **expert**	Enid is an **expert** in bowling, so she will teach me. I am just a **novice.**
obliging (*adj.*) ə blī′ jing	ready to do favors; friendly; helpful; kind	Charlene will surely lend you her notes because she is an **obliging** person.
occasionally (*adv.*) ə kā′ zhən ′l ē	once in a while; now and then; sometimes	No one is perfect. Everyone makes a mistake **occasionally**.

occupation (*n.*) äk′ yə pā′ shən	work that a person does to earn a living; line of work; trade, business, or profession	Lola is a computer programmer, and her brother, too, is preparing for that **occupation**.
offender (*n.*) ə fen′ dər	person who does wrong or breaks a law; culprit	We were awakened in the middle of the night by someone singing loudly in the street. The **offender** was probably drunk.
optimist (*n.*) äp′ tə mist	person who is cheerful and believes that everything will turn out all right *ant.* **pessimist**	Chen lost his watch, but he is sure someone will find it and return it to him. He is an **optimist**.
otherwise (*adv.*) u*th*′ ər wīz	in all other ways	It was cloudy in the morning, but **otherwise** it was a pleasant day.
	if things were different	Pearl was ill. **Otherwise** she would have come to the meeting.
pastime (*n.*) pas′ tīm	pleasant way of spending spare time; amusement; hobby	Is watching TV your only **pastime**? Do you have any other hobby?
pause (*v.*) pôz	stop for a short time; hesitate	Before answering the teacher's question, Richard **paused** to collect his thoughts.
pedestrian (*n.*) pə des′ trē ən	person who goes on foot; walker	If you ride your bicycle on a crowded sidewalk, you may hit a **pedestrian**.
permanent (*adj.*) pur′ mə nənt	not temporary; lasting or meant to last for a very long time *ant.* **temporary**	The Pilgrims left England and lived for a time in Holland before finding a **permanent** home in America.

pessimist (*n.*) pes′ ə mist	person who expects things to turn out badly	The coach, who is an optimist, expects us to win. But my sister, who is a **pessimist,** says we will lose.
popular (*adj.*) päp′ yə lər	very well liked; having many friends and acquaintances	Marty is sure to be elected if he runs because he is one of our most **popular** members.
	liked by most people	Corned beef and cabbage is a **popular** dish.
practically (*adv.*) prak′ tik lē	almost; nearly; to all intents and purposes	At five in the morning, the streets are **practically** deserted.
principal (*adj.*) prin′ sə pəl	most important; main; chief	One of the **principal** things to do when you have a cold is to get plenty of rest.
(*n.*)	head of a school	If you do superior work, you will get a certificate of merit from the **principal.**

IMPORTANT: Note that **principal** can be used either as a *noun* (*n.*) or an *adjective* (*adj.*).

privilege (*n.*) priv′ ′l ij	special right	Membership in the public library gives you the **privilege** of borrowing books without charge.
prohibit (*v.*) prō hib′ it	refuse to permit; forbid *ant.* **permit**	The management **prohibits** smoking in certain parts of the theater.
readmit (*v.*) rē′ əd mit′	admit again	Once you get off the bus, the driver may not **readmit** you unless you pay another fare.
reappear (*v.*) rē ə pir′	appear again	The snake that slid into the bushes has not **reappeared.**

reapply (*v.*) rē′ ə plī′	apply again	A member who left the club a year ago is **reapplying** for membership.
rearrest (*v.*) rē′ ə rest′	arrest again	The suspect who escaped from the police has been **rearrested**.
recall (*v.*) ri kôl′	call back to mind; remember *ant.* **forget**	I was not able to open the lock because I could not **recall** the combination.
	call back; cause to return; order back	Last January, the company dismissed four workers. But it has just **recalled** them because business has improved.
recapture (*v.*) rē kap′ chər	capture again; retake	The defeated champion said she would try to **recapture** her title next year.
reconsider (*v.*) rē′ kən sid′ ər	consider again; think about again	After saying I would not go to the game, I **reconsidered** my decision and bought a ticket.
recover (*v.*) ri kuv′ ər	get back; regain	Watch your belongings. If they are stolen, you are not likely to **recover** them.
	get well again	You have not completely **recovered** because you still cough a bit.
reenter (*v.*) rē′ en′ tər	come back in again; enter again	The firefighters did not permit the tenants to **reenter** the smoke-filled building.
reexamine (*v.*) rē′ ig zam′ ən	examine again	The physician will ask you to come for another visit if he has to **reexamine** you.

reintroduce (*v.*) rē′ in trə dyoos′	introduce again; present again	After his bill was defeated, the senator said he would **reintroduce** it next year.
rejoice (*v.*) ri jois′	feel joy or delight; be happy	Our defeat in the championship game grieves us, but the victors are **rejoicing**.
relish (*v.*) rel′ ish	take pleasure in; like; enjoy	I try to do my work right the first time because I do not **relish** the thought of having to do it over.
reluctant (*adj.*) ri luk′ tənt	unwilling; slow to act because of unwillingness; not inclined *ant.* **willing**	We had such a good time at the party that we were **reluctant** to leave.
renovate (*v.*) ren′ ə vāt	make new again, or like new; restore to good condition	It is generally cheaper to **renovate** an old house than to demolish it and build a new one.
reopen (*v.*) rē ō′ p'n	open again; begin again; resume	When is the show **reopening?**
reservoir (*n.*) rez′ ər vwär	place where water is collected and stored for use	The recent heavy rains have almost filled the town's **reservoir**.
	place where anything is collected and stored	Computers are **reservoirs** of facts and information.
reside (*v.*) ri zīd′	live (in or at); have a permanent home	Before moving to Houston, we **resided** in Baltimore.
respond (*v.*) ri spänd′	answer; reply; say something in return	Consider the question carefully before you **respond**.
	act as if in answer; react	When the store announces a sale, customers **respond** by buying up almost everything on the counters.

Dictionary 167

resume (*v.*) ri zōōm′	begin again	The rain stopped for a while, but soon it **resumed**.
	take again; occupy again	I got up to open a window, and then I **resumed** my seat.
reunite (*v.*) rē′ yoo nīt′	bring together again; unite again	The lost child was **reunited** with her parents.
reveal (*v.*) ri vēl′	make known	When we have good news, we are eager to **reveal** it. When it is bad, we may conceal it for a while.
revive (*v.*) ri vīv′	bring back to life or consciousness; make strong again	The plant looked dead when she brought it home, but she was able to **revive** it.
rival (*n.*) rī′ v′l	person who tries to do better than another, or strives for a goal that only one can reach; competitor	Holly was elected because she made better speeches and had more posters than her **rival**.
rumor (*n.*) rōō′ mər	story or statement circulating from one person to another without proof as to its truth; unconfirmed report; hearsay	The mayor's absence from an important meeting led to a **rumor** that he was very ill.
scarce (*adj.*) skers	hard to get; not plentiful; not abundant *ant.* **abundant**	Water is **scarce** in countries where there is not enough rainfall.
seldom (*adv.*) sel′ dəm	not often; rarely; infrequently *ant.* **often**	You are very obliging. You **seldom** turn down anyone who asks for a favor.
select (*v.*) sə lekt′	pick out; choose; take in preference to others	A librarian can help you **select** a book to read in your leisure.

shy (*adj.*) shī	not at ease with other people; bashful	Laura was glad to meet the visitors, but Eric remained in his room because he was **shy**.
	easily frightened; timid	The pigeons became less **shy** when we offered them food, and they moved closer to us.
similar (*adj.*) sim′ ə lər	almost but not exactly the same; much the same; alike, like	Janet and Jeanette are **similar** names.
		Milton and I get along very well because our ideas are **similar**.
sincere (*adj.*) sin sir′	real; not pretended; honest	The jokes I told were not too funny, but the audience laughed to be polite. It was artificial laughter. It was not **sincere**.
strenuous (*adj.*) stren′ yoo wəs	needing much energy or effort; arduous	Shoveling snow is **strenuous** work.
superior (*adj.*) sə pir′ ē ər	better than average; very good; excellent	Most of the pupils scored between 75 and 80, so your 92 is a **superior** mark.
temporary (*adj.*) tem′ pə rer′ ē	lasting for a short time only; not permanent	My brother was unhappy to learn that his assignment to the mail room was permanent. He had hoped it would be **temporary**.
timid (*adj.*) tim′ id	easily frightened; feeling or showing fear or shyness; afraid *ant.* **unafraid; fearless**	If Martha had been more sure of her answer, she would not have given it in such a **timid** voice.
undecided (*adj.*) un′ dī sīd′ id	not sure what to do; hesitant	Have you made up your mind about how to vote, or are you still **undecided**?

		not settled; not decided	The date for the picnic is **undecided**.
unfamiliar (*adj.*) un′ fə mil′ yər		not familiar; not well-known; strange	At first, the neighborhood was **unfamiliar** to me, but I soon got to know it.
unruly (*adj.*) un roo′ lē		hard to control or manage; not obedient; disorderly	The **unruly** pupil was allowed to return to class after promising to obey the rules.
valley (*n.*) val′ ē		area of low land between hills or mountains	When the snow melts in the mountains, it swells the streams and rivers in the **valleys** below.
vanish (*v.*) van′ ish		pass suddenly out of sight; disappear *ant.* **appear**	The moment my back was turned my purse **vanished**.
		pass out of existence; cease to exist	The herds of buffalo that used to roam our plains have **vanished**.
victim (*n.*) vik′ təm		person who is injured or killed	One of the **victims** of the hit-and-run driver is still in the hospital.
		person badly treated or cheated	When there is dishonesty in government, the people are the **victims**.
victor (*n.*) vik′ tər		person who wins a contest, struggle, or battle; winner *ant.* **loser**	Thomas E. Dewey seemed to have won the 1948 election for President, but the final count showed that the **victor** was Harry S. Truman.
wholly (*adv.*) hō′ lē		completely; altogether; entirely	Most of the buildings were damaged by the hurricane. A few were **wholly** demolished.